WHEN DIVORCE HITS HOME

Other Avon Books by
Beth Baruch Joselow

LIFE LESSONS:
50 THINGS I LEARNED FROM MY DIVORCE

WHEN DIVORCE HITS HOME

Keeping yourself together when your family comes apart

BETH JOSELOW & THEA JOSELOW

AVON BOOKS ◆ NEW YORK

WHEN DIVORCE HITS HOME is an original publication of Avon Books. This work has never before appeared in book form. The stories herein are true. Names and places have been changed to respect the privacy of the families involved.

AVON BOOKS
A division of
The Hearst Corporation
1350 Avenue of the Americas
New York, New York 10019

Copyright © 1996 by Beth Baruch Joselow and Thea Joselow
Published by arrangement with the authors
Library of Congress Catalog Card Number: 95-41676
ISBN: 0-380-77957-9

Library of Congress Cataloging in Publication Data:
Joselow, Beth.
    When divorce hits home : keeping yourself together when your family falls apart / Beth Baruch Joselow and Thea Joselow.
        p. cm.
1. Children of divorced parents—Psychology.   2. Children of divorced parents—Attitudes.
3. Divorce—Psychological aspects.   I. Joselow, Thea.   II. Title.
HQ777.5.J67   1996   95-41676
306.874—dc20   CIP

First Avon Books Trade Printing: March 1996

AVON TRADEMARK REG. U.S. PAT. OFF. AND IN OTHER COUNTRIES, MARCA REGISTRADA, HECHO EN U.S.A.

Printed in the U.S.A.

QM   10   9   8   7   6   5   4   3   2   1

This book is dedicated to the memory of The Dingle, faithful escape vehicle—Datsun 210, 1980–1993

Acknowledgments

This book is the result of years of living, learning, loving, and observing. It is dedicated to all the people I can't live without: Ethan, Gabini, Dad, Tom, the Grandparents Baruch, the Joselows, Rosie, Jessie and Sarah, the uncles and the aunts, Nerie and Nestor. It is also dedicated to the people I would never want to live without: the Dink Tank, Burchman, Skills, Jeff, Fritz, Hillary, Allison, Jessie, Scooby, Greg, Studebaker, Adam, Kristen, Mindy, Bippy, all the Obies, and all the people who let me pick their brains. Special thanks to Oberlin College, which gave me course credit for writing this book. Finally, let me thank my mom for both having and putting up with me. We learned a lot about the both of us doing this together. It was the best divorce therapy possible. I wouldn't have wanted to do it myself.

Thea Joselow

Thanks, above all, to Thea for being so smart, so loving, and so much fun, and to the people whose stories make up this book. You are brave, caring, and wise. Thanks to my sons, Ethan and Gabe, who are two of the wisest and funniest people I know. And much thanks to friends and relatives whose care makes everything feel like it matters: Tom, Jessica, and Sarah Mandel; Ric, Sylvia, and David Baruch; Cindy Sheffield, Bryna Gollin, Maxine Clair, Carole Stover, Alice Powers, Rangeley Wallace, Mary Truitt, Terry Braunstein, Noah Alan Harris, Rosanne Faust, Marie Scarfi, Paul Genega, Jim Werkowski, and Tina Darragh.

Beth Joselow

Contents

Note to Children of Divorce

This is not a book for people who are getting divorced. This is not a book for the lawyers, friends, or pets of people who are getting divorced. This is a book for the children of people who are getting divorced. You didn't have any say in whether it was a good idea for your parents to get married in the first place, and more than likely you were not consulted when they decided not to stay married. You were, however, directly implicated in the whole thing. Why shouldn't you have a book just for you?

When my parents got divorced there were books to tell them all about personal issues, legal issues, money stuff, and how to deal with each other and how they were feeling. But there was nothing in the whole pile of divorce information to tell me what to do or how to feel better. There you have the origins of this book. I had to run all over the place, harass countless friends and acquaintances and tape what they had to say to gather the bits of advice that are now so neatly compiled be-tween these covers.

You don't have to read this book from beginning to end. You probably won't need answers to questions in the precise order in which we present them. Flip through, see what catches your eye, take from it whatever you want. There is no right or wrong way to go about it. This wasn't written by a psychol-ogist, an attorney, a teacher, or a social worker. This whole thing was done by a college student with divorced parents and her mother—the author of a book for women on divorce—and made possible by a computer, an overused phone, and the many smart, pulled-together people who allowed the two of us to interview them. The people we spoke to have been through some very tough times, as you will see. But they have all gotten through them, in most cases with wisdom and grace. They're out in the world now, going to school, working at jobs, partying with friends, making goals for themselves. They are not *victims* of anything. They are people in charge of their own lives.

Divorce is hard. But you'll get through it. I hope this book helps you over some of the rough spots and then some. Let me know.

Thea Joselow

Note to Separated and Divorced Parents, Teachers, and Other Interested Adults

This book is an inside view of divorce, from the kids' perspective. But it is not meant only for kids. Anyone who is interested in the welfare of children who are going through a family divorce can learn a lot from what the people here have to say.

It seemed only natural after writing a book for women in the midst of divorce to look to the stories of their children. Here at home, I could see in my own three children that divorce was a complex learning experience for kids, and one that they could have used more help with. Many of my students at The Corcoran School of Art are from divorced families and they, too, demonstrated that their parents' divorces had been a significant and troubling passage for them.

Divorce is a sad event. It is unfortunate, but often it is better than the alternative. If you look at the stories here, it is evident that the kids who suffered most were suffering long before their parents divorced. The problems raised by divorce are often just clarified versions of problems that marriage helped to hide. A parent with a drug or alcohol problem becomes much more visible when the partner who had helped mask what was going on lets go. A parent who has not made deep connections with his or her children while the marriage was intact is the parent who continues to let the kids down after separation. Angry people may have been seething for years inside of a marriage that wasn't working. Their children were already feeling that anger. In short, kids with deeply troubled parents will suffer whether their parents remain together or not. It is only the terms of the suffering that change.

When Thea and I began to talk to the kids of divorce, we found they were eager to tell their stories, especially if they thought their stories could be of help to other people. They had absorbed a great deal. Most of the time they had coped without the aid of support groups, regular counseling, stable home lives, or consistent attention from wise and caring adults. They leaned where they could lean. Usually that was on their friends. Kids can be really good to each other.

Some of the people we talked to had become adults very rapidly, assuming adult responsibilities that many of us would find daunting. Some experimented with all kinds of self-destructive behavior, because they did not know of other ways to escape the pain they were feeling. They just wanted to turn it off.

But the people who share their stories here are people who have come through their parents' divorce with something gained. We had no shortage of people to talk to. We decided to limit our interviews to young people ages 16 to 28, who would be closest in age and experience to the audience we were writing for. We also wanted to get the stories of people who had overcome much of the hardship that divorce had brought with it. All of the young men and women we talked to are doing well today—taking care of themselves in the real world of school and/or jobs. Most of them have come to terms with their less than perfect families. Few of them retain the illusion that families *can* be perfect.

What strikes me most is how little they seek to place the blame for what they've been through on their parents. They understand how hard it is for some people to be as good as they might want to be. They care more about healing themselves than they do about finding someone to blame for their pain.

Some of our interviewees have achieved more wisdom and stability than others. These are almost always the ones who had at least one stable, responsible parent behind them all the way through.

We adults can learn a lot from this generation of children of divorce. They are very direct in telling us what they need from us and what they have not always gotten. They understand that life is a complicated business, that divorce brought new problems into their lives, but that no one's life is problem-free. They would have had some of their problems with or without divorce.

Although Thea and I are not sociologists or psychologists or professional theorists, we are personally experienced with divorce, as well as practiced observers. What we have seen tells us that as tragic as divorce is, it is a necessary solution to certain problems. It is a mistake to blame divorce for the burdens that we place on our children much too soon in their lives. Parents who have never grown up themselves, or who cannot manage their own enormous burdens, make difficulties for their children both inside and outside of marriage. In fact, the end of a marriage can sometimes lighten the load.

What can we do to help the large number of kids who are growing up too much on their own? Read their advice to each other here. They will tell you.

Beth Joselow

It's Not Your Fault

It is not a bad thing that children should occasionally, and politely, put parents in their place.

—COLETTE

It's not your fault. This is, or should be, the first thing your parents tell you. That doesn't mean you will believe it. They will say other things along the way that might make you think it's at least partly your fault that your family is splitting up. Chances are they will say things that make you think that even if the actual divorce isn't your fault, life would be easier for them if you weren't an issue.

What's really going on here is that your parents are unfortunately involving you, the child, in their mental process of trying to work out what they are supposed to do. They are bound to be upset and confused themselves, so it really isn't surprising that they might say and do things that don't make the best kind of sense.

There isn't a kid out there with divorced parents who hasn't thought about what part he or she might have had in bringing

1

on the divorce. The possibility that you could have been the cause of the complete breakup and restructuring of your family is a very heavy thought. It's also just not true. It's unlikely that anyone else is going to accuse you of this awful deed, so you have got to stop accusing yourself.

All you can do is try to put such negative and destructive thoughts out of your head. Admittedly, this can be easier said than done (no kidding!!). Sometimes, even if your parents don't say anything directly about your part in the divorce, it can seem as if they are suggesting that you were part of the problem. Maybe you've overheard them arguing about how you're doing at school or who your friends are. They may have real concerns about you, but these are not the reasons that their marriage did not work out. If they're saying things that hurt you, tell them to stop. You will feel a lot better if you stick up for yourself.

There is no call for you to feel the least bit guilty. It is not your fault that two people who happen to be your parents have decided that they can no longer remain married, whatever their personal reasons might be. It is certainly not your fault that divorce has become a common event in contemporary life. You can't hold back the tide. You can only try to go with the flow.

- Tell yourself as much as you have to, "It's not my fault!" even if you have to repeat it 100 times a day.

- If anyone else does or says anything to make you think you helped bring about your parents' divorce, tell them, "It's their divorce. It's not my fault!"

- Remember that feeling guilty won't do anybody any good, least of all yourself. Anyway, you have nothing to feel guilty about.

When I was 15, on September 9, my father was sitting at the dining room table. My parents had been arguing. He told me he was moving out. Now, he hadn't told my mother, so this was the first time she was hearing it also. I remember thinking that it was my fault because I had gotten into a huge argument with my father that day, and I thought that it was the last straw, that I had pushed him over the edge. And I had told him that day, "I don't want to live with you anymore. I'm tired of living with you." And so, whether it was coincidence or whatever, I don't know. But I felt really guilty. I remember not being able to sleep. I just felt really responsible.

PAM, Age 19

Once, at Halloween, my parents got into a huge argument about my costume. It was like five o'clock and I didn't have a costume and my mother said she had told my father to take care of it and he said he didn't remember her saying anything about it. So I didn't have a costume. I was like eight years old at the time. And they got into some kind of big screaming match about it. Like one of those "you always" and "I never" fights where they were calling each other names and getting really hot. I don't remember exactly what I did about Hallow-een, but I think we threw some kind of thing together for me and I went out with the other kids on our block. About a couple of weeks later, my dad moved out and my mother told me they were going to get a divorce. For a long time I thought it was about my Halloween costume! I really hated Halloween for a couple of years. I would dress up and go out, but I'd be feeling really down. I never asked either one of my parents to help me with my costume, that's for sure. Of course, now I realize that nobody would get divorced because of a Halloween costume, not even a really cheesy Halloween costume! But it was hard for me to just get it—that I had nothing to do with what went on between them and I had just gotten caught in the middle of something. When I stopped feeling responsible for it, everything got a lot lighter and easier for me.

BEN, Age 16

I thought that it was my fault that they weren't getting along. When I was really little, like six or eight, I used to try to convince myself that they really did love each other and they were just acting like they didn't for my sake so I would grow up faster or something. I had it worked out in my head that it was all an act, and when I was older they would tell me that they really did like each other and they really were happy to be married to each other. Because I realized that when parents get divorced you grow up faster and I had this whole thing in my head that it was all to make me grow up faster. So it was much more pressure on me before the divorce than during it and after.

BETSY, Age 18

2

They're Both Still Your Parents

Nobody who has not been in the interior of a family can say what the difficulties of any individual of that family may be.

—JANE AUSTEN

Kids worry about so much when their parents get divorced. Sometimes they are afraid of things that their parents wouldn't even dream were in their kids' heads.

Right away it should be clear that it's going to take quite some time, years in some cases, for the children of folks who have divorced to figure out exactly what is going on in their relationships with their parents. Some patterns emerge fairly quickly. You know: when you see Dad and what you guys do together, what is more Mom's territory, that kind of thing. But inevitably there's a kind of awkwardness that lasts at least as long as it takes to work out these new patterns and habits. Why wouldn't it be awkward to suddenly have the most basic relationships in your lives undergo radical change?

You may find, oddly enough, that you become closer to your

father now that you see him less, because when you do see him he is more focused on you. The time that you spend with your mother may start to feel more significant because you are talking about things that matter more often. Things that your parents used to talk about with each other they may now discuss with you. Mom may talk to you about the people and problems she's dealing with at work, rather than telling Dad at night after you go to bed. You may go on the errands with Dad that Mom used to go on. Relationships are going to change. But they are both still your parents.

Except in extenuating circumstances, you will still have a mom and a dad. They don't live under the same roof anymore and they may not behave the way you think a mom or a dad should behave, but you were born with two parents and that's who they will be until the end of time. Each of them has contributed to creating the unique person that you are. Each of them has a significant role in your life, whether or not they live up to it. Let's hope they do. Even when stepparents enter the picture (more about that later), they are additions to the parental unit, not replacements.

People sometimes find that they become much closer to one parent. Sometimes they even lose contact with the other. Not a good idea. So if it's within your control, stay in touch with both of your parents, even if it doesn't feel natural and easy, even if you're mad at one of them. Once you cut someone out of your life, it's really hard to get things started again, so you really ought to keep that motor running.

If there are special circumstances or feelings that would make it harmful or not in your best interest to maintain close contact with a parent, you will, regrettably, have to deal with that loss. Even if your parents try to look out for you and try to make things easier, you are the only one who can really engineer the new relationships you have with them from this point on. Be reasonable—don't go off in a huff. You may regret that later. But if you have good reason to stay clear of one of your parents, be honest about your feelings and get support for your decision from adults who can be helpful to you. Do you have relatives, other than your parents, you can turn to? Teachers? Other adult friends?

Young kids usually seem to think that their parents are omniscient, all-powerful, semiperfect beings. Even if you'd already brought them down off that pedestal, whatever illusions you still had about their stature have been shattered. They probably look more like a pair of confused people than Supermom and Superdad these days. If your parents behave strangely when they separate and don't seem able to give you what you need just when you need it most, remember that neither one of them is divorcing you. Even if you live with just one of them now and never spend so much as a night at the other parent's place, he or she is still your parent, too. Who knows, maybe if you keep reminding them that that's who they are, they will remember to act like a parent more often.

- No one has divorced you.

- All parents make mistakes. Married ones can hide them better.

- You may become closer to one parent than the other. That's okay. Don't feel guilty about what happens naturally.

From a selfish point of view their divorce benefited me in almost every possible way. I became infinitely closer with both parents than I'd ever been when they were together, because neither one of them really had to deal with the other one anymore and so they just focused on me. My parents are my two best friends now. I was always close with my parents, but I don't think I'd have the relationship I do with them now if they hadn't gotten divorced. They'd always concentrated on me, but now each of them concentrated solely on me and really sought to establish that kind of relationship. For me, I benefited except for a few minor things, like who are you going to spend Christmas with and that kind of stupid thing. My advice to parents would be to do it the way my parents did. Make sure your kids know that your divorce has nothing to do with them and make sure that you concentrate on the kids. Because chances are you've been concentrating on each other and trying to make things work for however many years. Now that you're done and you're getting divorced and you don't have to deal with the other person anymore, spend your effort concentrating on your kids because they're going to need you.

NICK, Age 20

I saw my dad once a week, usually during the week. He'd pick me up after school and I'd go to his house and then he would bring me to school the next day. And it was never any big visitation thing. My parents never said bad things about each other to me. It was really nice. Until I got older. When I was in school and stuff they never talked bad. I knew that my father didn't like how my stepfather treated me, but he would never say anything, and my mom never said anything bad about my dad. I do remember, everybody makes these kind of lame state-ments to their mom. You know, like, well what if I wanted to go live with Dad? Even if you don't really mean it, you feel bad that your dad's over there by himself. My grandmother tells these stories to anyone who will listen. One of them is, "She was on the potty and she was so sad and she said,

'Granny, I miss my daddy, I know he's so lonely.' And we just were crying." Everybody thinks their dad needs them. You miss him. I don't think that realistically I would ever have wanted to live with him.

JILL, Age 28

3

Divorce Is a Change, Not the End of the World

One never knows what will happen if things are suddenly changed. But do we know what will happen if they are not changed?

—Elias Canetti

Okay, divorce is a big deal. It does mean that life as you know it is over, but if you'll allow some amateur philosophy for a moment, the end of each day of your life also means that life as you have known it is over. Every day that we're alive brings change.

Divorce is not necessarily major demolition for you. It is just the reorganization of almost everything. This reorganization may run the gamut from where you have dinner on Tuesdays to who's paying for your jeans and how. Life is likely to be pretty inconvenient until you get some kind of pattern going. Accept this. You are going to have to deal with the changes, and you can make them work for you.

10

Your parents will probably try to make all of these changes as easy as possible, for themselves and for you. Of course, their efforts may not always be successful and may not give you what you need. The shifting of responsibility, changes in scheduling, and other immediately apparent stuff will make things a bit inconvenient and awkward until you guys all get it together for yourselves and each other. The possible addition of a new pseudo-family can make things especially odd. Most of the people we've talked to about their parents' divorces use the words "weird" and "strange" a lot. If you have ever watched a movie with really choppy, artistic cuts from scene to scene you have some idea of what I'm getting at. It will be strange for you the first time Dad picks you up at rehearsal and drops you off behind Mom's house. It may be awkward at your graduation when you have to go from one side of the auditorium to the other to greet both sides of your family.

Change is not necessarily bad. Some people find that their relationships with their parents change for the better. They notice that they get a lot closer to the folks when the folks aren't working together in the "traditional" kind of family way. As you take on more responsibility and adapt to the new way that things are going to have to work, you learn about yourself and those around you. It's kind of like moving to a new house that you didn't help choose. Nothing is going to look familiar. The tile that you loved so much in the bathroom is suddenly replaced by hideous wallpaper that you never would have chosen. But you do really dig the new kitchen. It's a matter of trade-offs, adapting and making the new, strange stuff feel more comfortable. Once you get used to it, it may not be all that bad.

• Change is a part of life, a pretty important part, actually.

- Give yourself time to get used to it, then deal with it and keep moving on.

- Some things are going to stay the same. Not everything will be totally bonkers. Take comfort in that.

I feel cautious about marriage. My parents met each other when they were in college and they got married before my mom was out of college. She was a senior. So it makes me very cautious. I think they just rushed into it too fast. Maybe I'll get married some day. If I ever get to the point where I'm thinking about marrying someone I'm going to take a step back and say, wait, am I doing what my mom did? I guess divorce would remain a possibility in my mind. Especially because now I know it's not the end of the world. When I was ten or so I thought it was the end, the end of life as I knew it. I used to pray and wish that my parents wouldn't get divorced and try to convince myself that they really loved each other even though they never got along. They got divorced when I was 16. By then I actually wanted them to get divorced and just get it over with. It is the end of life as you know it, but it's not the end. You're still going to have the same friends and you're still going to go to school and you'll still be the same person. You're just living differently.

BETSY, Age 18

I got used to my mother dating my stepfather. But dating was one thing, marriage is another. The day they got married, they got married in court, we went out to dinner that night and I was pretty quiet. And I feel bad for being that way because I'd told them, "Yeah, get married, that's great." But I was pretty quiet, I was a bratty kid. I didn't look too happy and they knew.

But I got over it right away. I remember telling Mom before they got married, "Don't have children." Because we were her kids, I said, "Don't have kids." And she said she didn't think they would. I was reassured. Three months after they got married, they came to us and told us she was pregnant. And I blew up. And I didn't care if it was in front of him, I said, "You said you weren't going to get pregnant, you weren't going to have any more kids. We don't need any more kids in this house." I was very angry. But it's funny, six or seven months later, just like that, I was happy with the idea. I don't know what it was. The baby was born and for the first year or so I was so afraid of being so close to her, to love someone so much as I do because I was so afraid of losing it, like I'd lost my family and my father. I was afraid to fully love her. The second baby was a surprise. And I was very supportive of that. We were very happy. We all have our hands full.

LISA, Age 19

4

You Are Not Alone:
Just Look Around

Snowflakes, leaves, humans, plants, raindrops, stars, molecules, microscopic entities all come in communities. The singular cannot in reality exist.

—PAULA GUNN ALLEN

The day that you learn your parents are splitting up, you will probably feel like the only person in the world going through this whole thing. Rest assured, this is not so.

Open up a school directory one day; look at the names and addresses of the families and notice how many phone numbers are listed for each child. Let us put this into perspective: When an adult has multiple phone numbers it is indicative of some sort of mobility or success. Having a separate line in your car or in your pocket, having three office numbers and a pager, is a sign of being in demand. Children with five numbers listed next to their names are being passed around in a way that might feel familiar. The people responsible for them can be reached in more than one location. A kid with more than one phone number who has to memorize which day is attached to which parent and which phone is a kid who knows what you are going through.

Sometimes it seems like there are more people with divorced or otherwise not married parents than there are in "normal" family situations. Listen up: There is no such thing as a normal family anymore. There are so many different situations, many of them fully functional and healthy, that there is no kind of single definition of a family. The English language (wonderful tool that it is) has not changed rapidly enough to include vocabulary to describe every situation. Most kids out there do not, in fact, come from a suburban family with two and a half children, a dog, two cars, and a house with three bathrooms. It is a simple fact; in spite of what TV shows us, very few people are actually living that way. If you are, more power to you. That's super, and we wish you all the best in the world. Let us remind you, however, that even falling right into the ideal category does not obligate you to be happy all the time. You too have your problems and we understand that.

Meanwhile, for all the people who do not inhabit such a scenario, let us assure you that you are not alone. Look around your school, look around in traffic, look around in stores, and look to all your friends and acquaintances. Chances are that a goodly number of them have been directly implicated in someone's divorce. Some of those situations were much, much worse than yours. Some were much, much better. None of them was exactly like your situation. Each of those kids has a unique story, too, but you certainly have much in common.

Hey, check this out. I'll bet you never expected to see this: They all survived, too. Wow. Kinda gives you hope for the future, eh? Not only did they survive, many of them are pretty interesting, nice, understanding people to boot.

- Okay, they're not all nice, but who is?

- Look around before you jump to conclusions and start thinking that you are the only person going through this. Ask around, too, while you're at it. Other people sometimes have good advice.

- Try to help us out with the vocabulary to define the family of this new generation. Spread some slang.

My mom had always asked me if I wanted to go to counseling. She still goes, to group meetings and stuff like that. She asked me if I want to go now. I say no, no. I guess it might be cool to go sometime, but I'd go and I'd really not get into it. The counselor would try to talk to me and I wouldn't be like spilling my guts or anything. I just didn't have anything to say. I had friends but I never really talked about it with them. One of my best friends, Rudy, he just lived with his dad. We never really talked about it, but we hung out a lot for a long time because we related real well. I remember his dad always had girlfriends and stuff and I could tell it bugged him, too.

CHARLIE, Age 21

I never felt weird around my friends because everybody's parents were divorced. I think my boyfriend is the only one I know whose parents are still together.

DONNA, Age 20

I knew two girls when I was about six years old who both had parents who were divorced. They went back and forth between their parents' houses, a month here, then a month there. I didn't want to do that. It was fine for their parents to be divorced, but I didn't want my parents to be divorced even though I knew they weren't right for each other and shouldn't be together. But I just wanted them to stay together.

BETSY, Age 18

5

Your Parents Will Be Crazy for a While: It Gets Better

Until the rise of American advertising, it never occurred to anyone anywhere in the world that the teenager was a captive in a hostile world of adults.

—Gore Vidal

Just think about how out of control you feel about this whole divorce thing. Take that feeling and add to it the responsibility of children, a whole lot of guilt about having a marriage come to an end, the need to figure out how to organize a whole new life financially, socially, personally and emotionally. Yeah, your parents seem to have a reason or 12 to be a little bit bonkers around the edges.

Your parents are going to seem especially loopy to you as they try to figure out how to work out a lot of stuff that they had previously taken for granted and which seemed to work out naturally. Money is going to have to be distributed creatively; social stuff changes drastically when someone becomes

18

suddenly single; extended family relations are liable to be filled with tension for a while.

When you watch your parents experiment with solving all their new problems, you may think they are acting a bit crazed, unnatural, or absolutely insane and impractical. It is even possible that they might actually lose their grip on reality as we know it for a while as their lives, not to mention yours, change rapidly and in ways they couldn't have anticipated.

You are probably seeing your parents in a new light. You will notice more and more that they have no idea what is going on themselves. Most parents, when pressed, will admit that they still don't know what they want to be when they grow up. It may come as a surprise, if you are accustomed to seeing a united parental front complete with clue and plan, that they don't know *how* to get divorced any more than you know what you are supposed to do in this kind of situation. They are in new territory, too. If they've long been used to being in control of their lives, they may go especially strange in the face of so many things they *can't* control, and they may be shocked or ashamed that things have not worked out the way they had planned.

Whether you notice it or not, you yourself are probably doing some pretty strange things as well. Think about it: Did you used to wander around the city at three in the morning just to get some air before your folks separated? Did you decide to shave off half your hair before or after they went to court? We all can get kind of wild when big, confusing, annoying, painful, difficult things happen to us.

There just isn't a master plan for people to follow when they are going through a divorce. Even people who have been through it before don't know how it's going to work out *this* time. There isn't a happy way to do it, or even a right way.

Everyone just has to do the best they can to get through it without causing or feeling excessive and unnecessary pain.

Sometimes it may feel like the people who are supposed to be taking care of you have forgotten how to do that. Try to be patient with them, to walk around in their shoes a little bit before you disqualify them from the parents' hall of fame. You're right, of course, in thinking that because you are the child and they are the adults, they should be taking care of you instead of vice versa. But along with the fact that your parents have a lot of other things to deal with now, we all know that kids have a tendency not to communicate all that well with their parents. Now, especially, they could probably use some filling in on what their kids are thinking and feeling.

Communication has been a problem between parents and kids for as long as there have been families. It just gets a little more complex when the issues are as dramatic and life encompassing as they are when a family is getting all mixed up and turned around. It will help if you try to make your needs and feelings clear to your parents.

- Crazy Parent Syndrome is temporary. It usually goes away as they begin to feel more in control of their lives.

- You are probably exhibiting some Crazy Kid Syndrome yourself, whether or not you've noticed it.

- Speak up instead of suffering in silence. Be clear about your needs and feelings.

My mother put us through a lot. We would all get together, like for Thanksgiving "for my grandparents' sake," and it would seem like we were all kind of a happy family, which wasn't true. My mother had moved out. I lived with my father.

It was mostly friendly, but these weird things would happen. That Thanksgiving we gathered and were putting up such a front for the older relatives. And we had a long driveway. My sister looked out the window and said, "What is that car doing at the end of our driveway?" And my mother said, "Oh don't worry about that car." And then she said, "Oh, I have to go, I have to go." And she pulled her car up next to that car and they drove off. With her boyfriend. And I thought, Why are you doing this at Thanksgiving? . . . I had so much angry feeling toward my mother. I didn't realize that at first. My mother would say, "Don't lay a guilt trip on me. I've never had my own life. I admit I'm a lousy mother and I just want my own life for myself now." What a great thing to say to your children! I didn't know quite what it was, why I felt so black. But I went to a counselor, I asked to go. And right away, when I walked into the waiting room for the first time, I just started bawling. I had so much stress about everything—about going to college, about moving. But it was mostly about my mother, about my hostility toward her. I still think it was a lousy thing for her to do. But I at least got a lot of it out. I didn't even know it was all there. It was terrible, the way she had chosen to leave. Not that it was directed at me, but with the counselor it grew into more of an understanding of the situation. Not an acceptance. Now I'm at a level with my parents where we all talk, we're all a family still. They're friends, we're all friends. They're still both my parents. They're not together, but it seems like today that's not so unusual. At least they get along.

KIMBERLY, Age 21

I think that my dad went through a mid-life crisis and he just never got out of it. It was like he moved out and he just got weird. He didn't used to be weird. . . . His moving out really affected my relationship with him and my sister's relationship with him. We used to get along well pretty well. And he just like moved out and was just completely enamored with this lady. And he spent all his time with her and we didn't get along with her. I think I'm being fair in saying that I wouldn't like her even if I had met her under different circumstances. And we'd go over there but it was really uncomfortable staying in her house. . . . I like my dad, I mean it sounds like I have this horrible thing with him. Our relationship is kind of strained and all, but I have a feeling that it will work out. I don't want to push it or whatever.

ERICA, Age 19

6

Don't Let Your Parents Put Each Other Down

I grew up to have my father's looks, my father's speech patterns, my father's posture, my father's opinions, and my mother's contempt for my father.

—JULES FEIFFER

Your parents probably aren't really fond of each other by the time they actually get around to getting divorced. This is the way it should be; people who still get along really well probably aren't the ones getting rid of each other. But just because they can't stand each other doesn't give either of them the right to tell you all about the flaws and foibles of the other. You are still related to both of them, and it is going to hurt to hear one of them saying unpleasant things about the other.

It may seem perfectly reasonable for your parents not to like each other. Whatever happened between them is bound to have left some bitter feelings. You may even like to be there for them as someone who cares about how they feel. It can

23

feel nice when your parents confide in you, when they tell you what's bothering them. But sometimes it gets to a point where you're being asked to be more than a good listener, where you have to hear things you don't want to hear.

You should have no qualms about telling your folks that you just don't want to hear it anymore. They should understand (especially after a little careful explanation) that you feel stuck in the middle. You don't like to hear bad things said about the people you love, and no matter what has happened you are still, technically, exactly half of each of them. By insulting each other, they are insulting you.

Remember, you're allowed to object to hearing your parents insult each other even if your relationship with one or both of them is strained. You don't have to feel loyalty or affection for your father to dislike hearing your mother tell you exactly what's wrong with him. No one ever said you had to be consistent. And you don't have to listen to disparaging speculations about your mother's way of life and how she went wrong whenever you spend time with your father. You have the right to protect yourself from having to hear about the things that went on between them.

Your parents' main connection to each other (aside from legal details) should be the child or children that they have in common. Letting them go on insulting each other to you isn't going to help anyone at all. Tell them you want them to respect *your* feelings until they learn to watch what they say about the people who you are related to. You are under no obligation to serve as an impartial counselor. They should be looking out for how you feel, and if they aren't, you should at least have total freedom not to listen.

Some people find that they can draw the line with their parents pretty easily, while others have a tougher time with it. Let it be said that your folks aren't psychic and that you should be able to verbalize how you feel diplomatically, i.e., without screaming and yelling or laying a big guilt trip on them. That would just make things worse for you. It is in your best interest to keep things open and honest without letting them get out of hand.

If it is easier not to mention the things that one parent does because it sets the other one off on a bashing spree, learn what you shouldn't mention.

It can get tough; you may feel like you are constantly defending one parent to the other, even after you have tried to draw boundaries. You may feel like your requests for a verbal cease-fire are being ignored. You may have to walk away, explain yourself every time the situation arises, keep drawing the lines that are always being crossed. Don't give up. Parents usually cool down after a while and won't continue to bash each other for life.

But if it seems like they are never going to run out of ammunition to use against each other when speaking to you, you may just have to close the subject. Saying, "Mom, I don't want to hear you talk about Dad anymore—at all, unless it is strictly necessary, and even then I just want the facts" is not exactly subtle, but it may help. You can cut them off as they begin; for example: "Your mother—" "Dad!!! Cut it out, don't even start." Again, you are not going to win any subtlety awards, but if they can't get the point you may have to go to the extreme. Hint: It never helps to reply to one parent with what the other one has said on the same subject. If your dad talks about how cheap your mom is, don't tell him that she says the same thing about him. This never works and it tends to get you in trouble.

- Your parents probably won't know when something bothers you if you don't tell them about it.

- You can listen to their problems without letting them talk dirt about each other; you are not a therapist.

- Don't fight fire with fire. You are not going to help out anyone, including yourself, if you alienate your parents.

What was really hard for me was trying to maintain a balance. It was hard to keep a relationship with my dad while my mom was really down on him. My dad wasn't like that with my mom, probably because he didn't have as much reason to be. She was really obnoxious and rude about it. I guess I try not to get in the middle. Difficult advice to follow; it's kind of hard to do. Just try not to let them put you in the middle. I mean, my relationship with my dad was already really messed up and it didn't help that my mom was down on him and I lived with her.

ERICA, Age 19

I didn't want to be around. I didn't want to feel like I had to mediate, and I should not have seen the things that I was seeing. So the way that I deal with it now is if my mom—it's usually my mom because I'm around her so much—she'll start talking about my dad and she'll start talking about how he's really pissing her off with the divorce, and I just say, "Mom, uh-uh, I don't want to hear it." It even got to the point where I said to her, "Would you not bring up Dad until I bring him up? We talk about him so much. It's not what I want to discuss." He's not what my life is about. He's definitely affected my life, but he's not everything that I am about and I don't want to spend all my time talking about him. I never knew the difference between being a child and being just sort of a third party, because you know, that's something very different.

PAM, Age 19

7

Don't Let Your Parents Use You as a Go-between

Never try to walk across a river just because it has an average depth of four feet.

—MARTIN FRIEDMAN

Usually when two people divorce they are not too enthusiastic about talking things over with the person they just divorced. All kinds of complex emotions, multiple tensions, anxieties, and assorted other nastiness combine to make them a bit edgy and uncommunicative with each other. Each one wishes the other would just go away.

So it's not surprising that ex-partners who have children in common, and therefore *must* communicate with each other, have the tendency to use the kids as message bearers. This is not meant to be cruel. It's just that if the kid is going to go see the mother anyway, why shouldn't he or she bring Mom that medical bill she owes Dad money for? Sounds very neat and clean, doesn't it? Just tell your mother that the check is late; you're going over there anyway, right? Well, why would you or anybody else want to be the bearer of bad news? It's fairly uncomfortable, possibly damaging to your relationship with one or the other parent, and really annoying. They're the adults. They should be able to work out their own financial stuff without using you as a carrier pigeon.

How does it feel when your parents don't want to talk to each other and prefer to send their messages through you? You don't have to refuse if you don't mind and if the messages are just routine. But a lot of people don't like to be put in the position of telling Dad that he owes Mom money for food or clothing or shelter, etcetera. If it makes you uncomfortable, if Dad ends up asking you when you get to his place, "What did she send this time?" if you just don't want to hear Mom say, "Give this to your father; you know I can't talk to him," you ought to just inform them that the post office sells these little things called stamps and if they affix one of these nifty devices to an envelope containing their little missives it will arrive (hopefully) in the hands of the opposite parent. You can tell them to use the phone, mail, or common friends. It is not up to you to deliver their messages.

There are other ways to deal with this. If the messages are always about your finances, you can take all of your bills into your own hands and communicate directly with each parent. This is not a method recommended for small children. If you aren't ready to take care of your own issues, you might want to help your parents work out a way to be in touch with each other that doesn't make you feel like a Ping-Pong ball or doesn't expose you to fits of rage that come down on you instead of on the person he or she is really angry with. You belong to both sides. Your family ties shouldn't be jeopardized or strained by your parents' inability or unwillingness to communicate.

If you don't mind delivering messages, go for it. It may make your life easier. You should also feel free to discriminate between what you will and will not convey. If you don't mind saying that it is your dad's turn to drive you home from school or to pick up the dental bills, go ahead. If you do mind, however, you need to be able to decline gracefully. You may need to explain this to your folks. Tell them where you draw the line, once you've worked that out for yourself. Figure out what makes you feel weird and what you don't mind and let them know. This is not to say that you need to draw up some kind of family manifesto that explains exactly and in detail what is okay and what isn't. You just have to know how you feel (not the simplest of assignments), and know how to communicate that in situations where in the past you've felt at a loss.

At the same time, as you grow older, you will be taking on more and more responsibility for your relationship with your parents. So even when it's uncomfortable, you are working on building communications skills with them, and that will come in handy.

- If you don't want to deliver messages, learn to say so, clearly and firmly. Not harshly—just communicate what you will and will not do.

- If you don't mind being a messenger, go for it and good luck. The choice is up to you.

- Be flexible. When it is most practical for you to deliver news, when it is important to you to do so, learn how to do it without putting yourself in the middle of other people's conflicts.

On the surface, it's all very nice and quiet between my parents. But since we all live in the same town, me and my sister have both been like the battleground on some occasions. We just get the negative sides. My parents won't really say to each other, "Well, you're doing this or that wrong." They turn to us and say, "Your father did this and this and this and that really aggravates me," or "Your mother called up and said this and this, and that really aggravates me." More often it was about money and who pays the bills. And with this next year of school coming up I just said finally I'm not going to take it anymore. I'm going to get all the bills myself and I'm going to tell each of them how much to give me. They are supposed to divide everything fifty-fifty. It is something that I should have done a long time ago. Bills for school, bills for housing, and any bills that they'd be responsible for I'm going to get and I'll just itemize them and say, look, give me a check for this much. When they do it themselves it's just an endless argument. It's easier for me in the end to just take care of it.

JOHN, Age 19

I think that their children are their only reason for talking now. They don't talk at all besides that. They talk about our finances, they talk about travel plans, things like that, like where they want to take us for Christmas if they want to take us anywhere. I've never really seen them around each other. They can deal with each other, like at my brother's high school graduation we had dinner together. It was kind of awkward but not really. My stepmother was there and it was pretty weird but they were both cool about it. They weren't hostile to each other. They didn't say much that was friendly, but they weren't hostile. They've never really talked to us about our finances in their agreement. They want to keep us separate from that, they want to make it as easy as possible for us. And I think they're right. It would be a lot more awful if I heard about it every time they got into a fight. They get into arguments at times because my father won't pay his half of the phone bill or my father won't pay medical bills or something like that. He gets caught up in his work and he forgets to do those things on time, and my mom gets angry and she says your father's not paying this, but she keeps it her battle.

TRICIA, Age 17

8

Expect to Feel Confused

I have seen the truth, and it doesn't make sense.

—UNKNOWN

Divorce is a mess. Surely you didn't expect to get through this monster without some confusion about what your role should be or how things were going to go.

Human relationships are confusing things, and if you think otherwise you must not have been paying attention. Your parents are surely confused by all the stuff that is going on. People don't get married with the intention of getting divorced. Now, no one knows exactly how things are going to work out. People can't really anticipate their feelings very well, but you should expect to feel a little clueless about everything that is going on until well after it has all settled down.

Actually, come to think about it, no one really ever knows exactly what went on when their parents decided to split; they just stop worrying about it.

"Expect to feel confused?" You're probably thinking, "Is that the best they can do?" Well, sometimes it helps people to tell them what they already know. Confusion may be the actual underpinning of life. And divorce is certainly at the top of the list of life experiences that include mandatory confusion. You may think that you know all about what is happening. If your parents are honest with you, then you might know more than most, but no one ever has the whole story. This is because there is more than one story for each divorce. It's fairly likely that each of your parents has a slightly, or very, different version of their marriage and the reasons it didn't work out. You are the kid; you didn't decide to get divorced, and even if you support the decision 100 percent you still don't have a whole lot to do with it. Confusion and lack of control are pretty scary things, but with time your life will settle into new patterns and you'll regain some semblance of control.

Eventually you should be able to figure out what you do and do not need to know. You will learn and have your questions answered (in some manner or another) about things that involve you, and you will probably figure out what you neither need nor want to know. Face it, there are some things about your parents and their marriage that are none of your business and that you will probably be better off not knowing, at least for the time being.

Rest assured that confusion about adult relationships is not confined to kids. Most adults are in the dark about relationships themselves. Have you watched TV lately? Have you gone to the bookstore? There are countless shows and shelves of books trying to explain to adults how they went wrong, what they should do to keep their mate, stuff like that. One thing to keep in mind: All of these sources contradict each other with enthusiasm and wild abandon. The adults eat it up. These books and TV shows exist because people are always watching. They don't know what to do and they assume that someone else does. They are wrong.

Every situation is different. You know more about yours than those other people do. You are the only one who can figure out what is going on. You are confused. What else is new? You should not be surprised or dismayed by confusion, it is a natural state. Get some advice that makes sense to you from people you trust, find some other people who don't mind if you rant and rave sometimes, mull things over in your own mind, and have faith that after a while you'll arrive on solid ground again.

- People who have all the answers are seldom any fun to be around.

- No one knows exactly what is going on all the time. If they say they do, they are lying.

- With time and possibly effort, you will become less confused or at least less bothered by it.

During my senior year in high school I knew there were problems with my mom and dad. I didn't really want to see it because I had so much going on in my life. I was president of a girls' club and I was in the student council and the art guild. I kept busy. I knew things were going on at home, but I just didn't want to face it. . . . My parents were fighting a lot more, or if they weren't fighting they just weren't talking. My dad was gone a lot more than usual. . . . Then one day I was in my bedroom and I heard my dad slap my mom. And I ran out of my bedroom and went to him and said, "Don't ever hit my mom again," and she was like, "I hit him back. Don't worry about it." I was so mad, so upset because I didn't know why he was hitting her. What was my mom doing? Then my dad said he was moving out and then my anger went to my mom.

I was so mad at my mom. I was like, why? It was my senior year in high school. My graduation was coming up. I hadn't had my braces off yet. I was so angry with my mom because I thought my dad wouldn't show up.

TARA, Age 23

I lived at home, but I spent two days a week with my dad. I still do. For the first six to eight months, a long time, every time I saw him I'd ask when he was coming home. And I realize now how incredibly hard that must have been for him. But I was ten years old and I didn't know any better. I didn't understand then what was going on. I mean, I understood my parents were having problems and my dad needed to go away for a while, so it seemed logical for me to keep asking every week, "When are you coming home, Dad?" I realize now that whatever my parents were going through that must have made it so hard for my dad.

NICK, Age 20

9

Find a Friend to Confide In

There was a definite process by which one made people into friends, and it involved talking to them and listening to them for hours at a time.

—REBECCA WEST

People tend to have to talk through the things that upset them. It is terribly cheesy, yet it's one of those things we can't escape: People like to talk about what is bothering them. This is not restricted to people who are going through major life-style changes, the way that you are, but it is just as true for you as it is for others.

Talking about the things that bother you is a good way to sort through it all in your own head. You should not necessarily look for answers from the people you talk to; chances are that there are no easy solutions to the problems you are facing. But having someone there to listen sympathetically is always helpful. By talking through your concerns you will probably become more comfortable and understanding of yourself and your feelings. It's one of the cooler things about human beings that just talking about something can help you to feel better about it even if you don't actually change your situation much.

Friends are, or should be, there for you. They are there to help you through your stuff, in exchange for which you should be happy to help them through theirs. Just because your friend's parents are still together does not mean that your pal doesn't have problems that are as serious and intimidating as yours. Buddies listen to each other. Everything in friendship should be a two-way street.

Try to choose your confidantes wisely. Some people can't keep anything to themselves. Whatever you tell them will be all over the Western Hemisphere in ten minutes. Those are not the people you should talk to about subjects that are excruciatingly personal. Resist the urge if it comes over you. Think of someone you know to be discreet.

Friends can do a lot for each other: They can provide escape, companionship, understanding, sympathy, caring, advice, a good laugh, a good cry, someone to argue with and someone to play with, someone to trust, and they are on your side no matter what. Learn to confide in and depend on your friends and be able to do the same for them. A good friend is priceless.

- You will probably want to talk to someone about how you are feeling: Enlist a good friend to talk and listen to.

- Be there for your friends, especially if you are depending on them to be there for you.

- Your friends may have problems that are just as serious as yours. Be sure to listen, too.

I didn't depend on people until about six or eight months after the divorce. I was just too bottled up inside and I didn't want to give it to anybody because I didn't know who I could trust. My next door neighbor's mom and dad went through a divorce the year before mine. We used each other as support. We used each other to keep ourselves happy. Just, you know, "What do you want to go do? Let's go do something," when we were both feeling really anxious. We didn't face our problems, we didn't run away from them. It was just being with someone who was going through the same thing that you were and being able to talk about the stuff that was going on in our lives as if we had normal lives.

TARA, Age 23

I did have an older friend, she was 40, who was a neighbor. We became friends when I was 12 and moved next door to her because her daughter would come to visit her in the summer. She was divorced. Then I just started hanging out with this woman a lot. And she, I would say, gave me anything that I had, any support that I had. I could talk to her about how I was feeling, but I don't know how much I did. I mean, I'm a pretty quiet person. She was the first person who ever talked to me like I was, you know, just a normal person, who acknowledged that I had a personal view, that I was around. That meant a lot. To be acknowledged.

LAURA, Age 22

Don't Be Afraid to Ask Questions

It is better to ask some of the questions than to know all the answers.

—JAMES THURBER

This is your life. You have every right to know about the things that will affect you for years to come. Why shouldn't you ask questions? You may wonder where you will live, about how your parents will get along now; you may not even be so clear on why they are breaking up. You have every right to ask the questions that plague you.

Keep in mind, though, that your parents may not always feel ready to answer. No doubt they need some time to deal with some of these matters before they feel all right about explaining them to you. And there are still things that are purely their business.

It would be nice if we could all communicate freely and openly, but it is seldom the case that anyone knows everything about anyone else. You must have things that you feel and think about that you wouldn't be able to fully explain to your folks. They have similar thoughts and feelings of their own. Everyone is entitled to some privacy, and we should respect each others' boundaries.

You are absolutely within your rights to ask any questions that you want to, and by the same token, they are perfectly within their rights not to answer all of your inquiries. You don't need to know everything about your parents' relationship before or after their divorce. They may not feel at ease discussing these things with you now—or ever.

At the same time, openness and honesty about things that affect the members of a family are important qualities in a healthy family. As time passes and your parents make some of their own adjustments, they may be more willing to talk. They are likely to be more open with you if you show that you can handle what they have to say. Sometimes they won't want to answer your questions because they are worried that the answers will upset you. Maybe you should talk about that, too.

Sometimes parents just tell you not to worry about it. That is the most efficient way to ensure that you worry about it until the end of time. It is nearly impossible to just stop worrying about something because someone tells you to. The way to stop worrying is to get an answer or explanation. Even if it is not a complete or ideal answer, it is better than avoiding the issue or declaring the topic off-limits. Tell them that you need to know.

In the midst of all this change, how could anyone think you would have no concerns? You would be kind of unusual if you already had all the answers. Who better to ask than the people who are supposed to raise and protect you, nurture you and mold your mind? After all, they are the ones who are at the center of this whole divorce thing, so they should know as well as anyone else what is going on. But if they are too caught up in their own private whirlwinds at the moment to focus on what you need to know, look around you. See if there is another close relative or friend who might be able to answer the questions that are keeping you awake at night. You'll sleep better.

- Ask questions. That's what kids are for. You get more answers that way.

- Your parents might not be able to answer you. It is annoying but allowed.

- Some things are not your business. Others are. Learn to tell the difference.

I asked my mom what happened to their marriage and she basically told me that when they were starting to see each other she thought he was one thing, but after they got married a few years later he turned out to be totally different. My mom was sort of an intellectual type who wore black turtlenecks. I don't know if that's putting someone into too much of a category, but she wore black turtlenecks and she read poetry and crusaded for equal rights for blacks and whites and so on. And my father was getting his PhD in economics and he came on as an intellectual type, which attracted her at the time. When she was dating him she was dating a couple other guys. I asked all this stuff and she told me. I was fairly pleased she told me. My father just kept being pretty steady about it, persistent. He bought her books and stuff. She likes stuff like that. Then after they got married she learned that he didn't really read any of this stuff. That strikes me as very odd. Why would you want to marry someone for not real reasons? I mean, on my father's side. I don't know if he was for real then either. And I've kind of tried to figure it out, but if I say, "Are you for real?" he'd get a little offended. And I sort of almost tried to say that a couple of times and he got really offended each time. So I decided not to ask him. It's not a nice thing to ask someone, but I really wanted to know because it was just eating at me.

REBECCA, Age 20

My dad this year will be 43. He is seeing a girl that went to school with me. I knew her in sixth grade. She used to try to beat me up all the time. He has two sons. One's a year old and she got pregnant when that baby was a month old. So I found that out last week. He didn't tell me. I found out about the other baby by mistake. My dad looks really old. He looks 20 years older than he is, really haggard. My family says, well, don't worry about it. But I'm not that way. I'm worried about it. Even with all the stuff he's done. My mom, well, in a way she's kind of selfish, she says, "There's things he's done that you don't know about because I was trying to protect you." And if I try to talk about them she always talks about what it did to her. She says, "Well, don't worry about it because there are so many things you don't know." It's almost the same speech every time, and I guess I get along with her, but if something happens, I call my grandmother. I don't really— I mean, my mother was like out of the equation.

MARIANNE, Age 25

11

Don't Blame Everything on Your Parents' Divorce

When I can no longer bear to think of the victims of broken homes, I begin to think of the victims of intact ones.

—PETER DE VRIES

Sure, divorce stinks. It creates endless problems emotionally and logistically for a good long time. Yeah, it is kind of a big deal, what with your whole family switching around and all, like a big complicated game of musical chairs. But keep in mind that this is not an excuse to slack for the rest of your life. Undoubtedly your parents split up because they thought that things would be better for all concerned if they no longer stayed together in a marriage that wasn't good for anyone. Yes, it's unfortunate, it's depressing, it's confusing and demoralizing. They only did it in the first place because they thought that things would be better if they were apart.

Keep in mind that every aspect of your success in life did not depend upon your parents when they were married. Why should everything focus on them now just because their relationship is changing? You cannot realistically blame everything that happens to you on their situation. If you fail a test it is not because your folks were talking to their lawyers. You need to ease up on them and take responsibility for yourself as much as you are able to. They probably feel guilty enough already, and no one likes a whiner.

This is not to make light of your emotional state. People have been known to become incapable of studying or doing assignments because they were distressed by things going on around them that they had no control over. There will be days like that, but you have to try not to let *every* day be like that. There are less painful ways of asking for someone to pay attention to you and your needs. One of those is simply to come right out and ask for help.

Experiment with putting the divorce out of your mind and getting on with your life. See whether you can change your frame of mind when you feel lousy. Bad things will happen to you. You will not win every race you enter, or get everything you want. You will fall for people who don't return your feelings or who don't treat you right. You won't always know what to do. Still, you cannot blame every loss or every bad relationship on the shenanigans of your parents. You can't put all of your problems on the shoulders of the divorce. Everyone has problems, and you would have had some no matter what.

At some point you have to decide that the victim role is elective—you don't have to play victim for the rest of your life. Try older but wiser survivor on for size.

You should be upset about the things that are going on. They involve you, they have an effect on you. But this divorce should not take over your life for the rest of your life. That is shortchanging yourself. You need to take care of yourself, keep a sense of having a life that is separate in many ways from your parents' lives, and keep some perspective on the things that are going on.

- It may be easier to blame everything on your parents' divorce, but it is hardly fair.

- You need to be responsible and not look for excuses.

- If you are angry, sad, or depressed, ask for help.

I think I actually drank a lot, in retrospect, which was really dumb. I don't know what I was thinking. I guess I was thinking, I don't want to deal with this. I had a couple of really bad incidents, things that made me want to check into a psych ward. I actually went to one, but then I didn't want to stay. But it was like a "Help, I'm drowning" kind of thing. I was kind of drowning. I was at the point where I . . . Well, I think my father's kind of nuts and I think that there's a little of that in me, too. I think I was kind of freaking out about it. I'm a lot stronger than that now. At that point it was, "Oh my God, I'm as crazy as he is." My father brought this up in court to show that my mother wasn't a good mother, the fact that this had happened to me. That was awful. It was a really hard time for me. I don't think it was fair of him to blame it on my mother because I wouldn't blame it on either one specifically but just on the way everything is closing in on you and you need to find your way out of it. My closer friends weren't particularly helpful at that point. Later I developed better friends, friends who were a lot more stable.

REBECCA, Age 20

I guess I had a problem with understanding relationships, one I might not have had if they hadn't been divorced. But I don't know. I never had the environment where I could say that my parents had always been together. I don't understand relationships in the way that someone else like that might. I understand relationships in the way that they take a lot of work and it's like people always say you need love and you need this and you need that, but you also need to put a lot of work into it because it's really easy these days to just say, "It's not working out. Stop." . . . It took more of a concentrated effort to figure out, because for years I thought things just happen the way they happen and I realize now that you have to make them happen. Things just don't happen. Things just happen, but they happen the way you allow them to happen. If you sit there and don't try to work out a relationship it will fall apart. If you sit there and work on the relationship you can make it stronger and better.

STEVE, Age 25

12

Get Used to the Idea That Your Parents Will Be Dating

I always knew I would turn a corner and run into this day, but I ain't prepared for it nohow.

—LOUISE MERIWETHER

Your folks have just undergone, or are still undergoing, the breakup of one of the central relationships in their lives. They have decided to give up the commitment they had made to the person with whom they had planned to spend the rest of their days. It's time to party! No, but they probably will date.

Not all separated or divorced parents date. Some find it too uncomfortable, distracting, or intimidating. But in most families, parents do turn up with new significant others. For some reason, one thing that can be observed in most families of divorce is that the kids tend to have more trouble with the people their mother dates than with those their father dates. Perhaps this is because most kids still spend more time with

Mom than with Dad, or because moms tend to make more of their lives known to their kids than dads do.

It is kind of strange to find your mom primping in front of the mirror because she is about to go out on her first date in 20 years. It is really odd to meet the people whom she brings home. You might feel kind of like you are interviewing for a job, with a lot of questions about just who is interviewing whom. You and the date are both scoping each other out, trying to imagine what problems you're likely to have with each other. Since dating is partly a testing of the waters to see if a relationship is feasible, the date is going to try to figure out if you are going to make trouble, take your mom's or dad's attention away, or if you can all be a happy temporary pseudo family. You, on the other hand, are trying to figure out if the date is going to sweep your parent off his or her feet and take away the attention that you have been accustomed to getting. And is this person going to embarrass you if your friends come over?

Kids feel strange when they see Mom acting like a gibbering teenager or Dad playing the adolescent gentleman. No matter how old people get, dating brings out the silliness in all of us. A lot of flirting and playing games goes on no matter what the ages of those involved. Chances are that your parents thought they had gotten out of that whole scene by getting married. They may feel silly and embarrassed about getting involved in it again, or they may go completely overboard with their first taste of frivolity in years. Either way, their behavior really isn't about you and certainly isn't meant to hurt you. They are just trying to find out what they want to do.

Sometimes what they want to do is in conflict with what you want them to do. Sometimes you may feel like you want to protect them from the creeps they come up with. The dating game really wasn't designed for people who are parents. The combination of families and organization of baby-sitters can get awkward, inconvenient, or just out of the question. You are going to take having dinner with Dad's girlfriend more seriously than he is. You will be more stressed because the situation is going to be strange for you, this bizarre new person sitting in Mom's place but who won't be there tomorrow. It's only natural for you to have problems with the whole situation. Seeing your parents date is a weird thing. You have been raised in a society where the order is: date, relationship, marriage, kids, death; not, date, marriage, kids, divorce, date, relationship. No one has told you how to feel about this; no one has set a precedent for what the "normal" way to relate to your parents' dates is. It's all pretty strange. You'll just have to learn to roll with it.

- Most folks are going to date. You won't get to choose who they date, either. Do they choose *your* dates?

- You may not like the people they come home with. As long as your folks don't try to force you to be too involved, this is okay. Just be polite.

- Some of the people your parents date could be pretty cool.

I actually didn't respect my father for a lot of the time that he was dating. I mean, in the first two weeks that they were separated he got a girlfriend. I remember very clearly when he met her. We were going to a dinner party at a friend's house and we got out of the car and there was a woman walking to the door with a bottle of wine. It was like a housewarming gift or something like that. I think he had a bottle of wine, too, and he said, "Oh, what kind did you get?" you know, and so that was the way that he met her. They didn't see each other very long. I think it was a just few months. But she had two children, so whenever they wanted to go out she would make me baby-sit. So I would drive with my father to go on his dates. He'd go to pick her up and leave me at the house. I didn't know any better. I was only 12. But I didn't like it.

TRICIA, Age 17

My mom had other boyfriends. Some of them were kind of cool. She had a couple that like played guitar and I could relate to them and they were kind of cool. Then she had one for a while who was kind of nerdy and I could not, I just felt like—it's weird, just because it was my mom, and I felt like she should have been with my dad or something. I always wanted her to be with someone who was better than the people she was with. Because she deserved it. She's cool. They always tried to have a relationship with me and it bugged me. It was cheesy. I did like the bike courier guy she went out with because he was chilled out, but he was older and he should have been into something that was making him some money. I don't know. He was okay for me, but not for my mother.

CHARLIE, Age 21

My stepfather had a very wild life. He's done everything. Now he's found this kind of simplicity and everything. It's amazing that he can just be satisfied with everything around him. He loves the routine, almost. I never had much trouble warming up to him or making an adjustment. It was the way my mom handled it. She didn't expose me to people that she was just dating. She only exposed me to him, who was the person she was really in love with. So I didn't have a problem with them getting married. I actually wanted them to get married because I saw how happy they were and it was real. Kids can feel when it's real love. And he had a definite love for me.

JOSH, Age 18

13

Some People May Be Really Insensitive

We want people to feel with us more than to act for us.

—GEORGE ELIOT

There are always people out there who are going to be insensitive. There are people who hate holidays and try to spoil them for everyone else. There are really selfish drivers. There are some people who always seem to have the wrong thing to say at important moments.

It could be that they just don't know what they should do and have no idea they are saying things that hurt you. Maybe they mean exactly what they are saying and it just doesn't match with what you think they should say. There are a million different varieties of insensitivity and there are just as many motivations for it. Your best option is to learn to take insensitivity for just what it is—something coming from *them*, not you. No one knows what is going on in your head or your life the way you do. People who act horribly or say stupid things shouldn't be taken too seriously.

People have been known to dismiss any personal problem as being due to your parents' divorce. Even when they may be right, that doesn't make it any less important to you. Teachers have told students that they are failing a class and then, in the same breath, blame it on the family situation. Even if that *is* what's up, the teachers are just explaining, not helping. It is their job to help you *not* fail. You might have to remind them of that.

The main problem is that divorce went mainstream so suddenly and relatively recently. There wasn't enough time to invent a protocol for dealing with all the issues and situations related to divorce that come up. What do you call your mother's second husband's first wife's kids? Is there such a thing as a stepgrandmother or a grandma-in-law? People don't know whether they should celebrate a divorce or mourn a marriage.

Of course, they might not have the best intentions to begin with. There is always the possibility that they are deliberately saying something bitter and unpleasant. Still, you are probably better off assuming that insensitivity is born of ignorance and awkwardness rather than malice. Your life will be easier if you avoid becoming overly sensitive yourself.

People sometimes take other people's divorces personally, as kind of a challenge. Yes, this is stupid, but it does happen. Friends will say something about how *their* parents were able to stay together, insinuating that your parents are defective. Even if you think your parents are defective, you don't want some outsider commenting on that. Relatives sometimes feel that their side of the family has been rejected by the other. Dad's parents may take it personally when their son is divorced by your mother. They might get bitter and say things that really hurt your feelings. They just don't know any better.

When dealing with people who are really insensitive to your situation and feelings, it is usually a good idea to be as tactful as possible. You can express displeasure at how people are acting without trying to claw their eyes out. Besides, clawing someone's eyes out is messy and illegal no matter how much they may deserve it. Try not to get too upset with people who just don't know what they are saying. It is bad for your blood pressure, and you are just reducing yourself to their level. As Ric Baruch (also known as Grandpa to Thea) always says, "Rise above it."

- People do and say stupid things all the time. It is not unique to your situation.

- Let's assume that they don't really mean to hurt you.

- Tell insensitive people that they are being insensitive without being accusatory or irrational. This is not always easy, but it's a worthy goal.

I went back once to see my stepfather a few years after the divorce. I found out where he was living and I drove about two hours to see him. I went up there about eight o'clock at night, and his new wife opened the door and she said, "He has a new life, leave him alone." And I said, "You know, that's kind of a stupid thing to say because I was a part of it for eight years. I just want to talk." And he came to the door and said, "Are you sure?" because he is kind of that way. And I said, "I remember something you told me: If I ever had anything I wanted to talk to you about, I could." And he looked at me and said, "All right. I'll come outside and talk to you." And we talked for a couple of minutes and I told him, "You were my father for like eight years." And he said, "Yeah, and I never really cared about you, did I?" And I said there were no hard feelings or anything. I was just up there tying up loose ends. Because I never got to say good-bye, and he didn't get to say good-bye. So he said, "Well, come in for a while." So I came in and we talked for about an hour and his wife was kind of hanging around. And I said, "It's cool, dude. Everything's all tied up. Have a nice life." I told him about what I'd been doing, and he told me since I obviously knew how to find him now I should let him know if I ever got anything together and wanted him to show up for a school thing or anything. Last I heard, he'd moved to California right after that. I think he freaked out over the whole situation. That was two years ago. There's a lot of aspects to that stuff that I don't deal with. I try not to deal with people who always ask me, "Is this all right?" "Is this all right?" I try to be very straight up, not rude, but no joking around. I can put up with anything else but that.

TIM, Age 22

For a long time I was going through a really bad period with my father, and other people would say, "Well, he's such an asshole" or, "He's a jerk." I'd get really defensive. But now I don't really mind. I'm very protective of my mom because I feel that she's been beaten up a lot. The only things that I've really heard directly about my mother have come from the mouth of my father's girlfriend, who is my mother's former best friend, or my father. So of course I'm going to be very defensive. There have been things said like, "Oh, of course she just couldn't let go." And I was like, "Well, excuse me. That's twenty-three years. How do you expect her to deal?" There was one stupid comment made by my former best friend, who is the daughter of my father's girlfriend, which made me realize I couldn't really salvage that relationship right now. She said to me, "Ever since our mothers haven't been friends, I feel like there's been a competition, and this is one point for my mother." I said, "I'm sorry, but my life falling apart doesn't get measured in points." That is almost not worth fighting because it's coming from someone so immersed in the situation that there's no way for her to be unbiased.

PAM, Age 19

14

Expect Some Changes in Your Living Arrangements and Life-style

Home. It's being new and old all rolled into one. Measuring your new against old friends, old ways, old places. Knowing that as long as the old survives, you can keep changing as much as you want without the nightmare of waking up to a total stranger.

—GLORIA NAYLOR

With your parents' newfound independence, assets are shifting. Finances are getting creative and costs are being divided up in new and interesting ways. Part or all of your family is sure to move to a different home and you may be trying to make it with less money. It is expensive to split one household into two or more. It costs more to live separately than together. These are facts, and unless you are very stable, things are probably going to change drastically for you.

There is no cure for your life changing. There is nothing that can be condensed into a paragraph or two to tell you how to keep your life from changing or exactly what to do about it when it does. You are just going to have to do the best you can with what you've got. Some people don't really mind the changes and adjustments that they have to make. They are willing and able to make the adjustments that are necessary to help their families begin a new life. They are from supportive families where people work together to make these changes more bearable.

Life, anybody's life, is change. It's just that kids whose parents don't divorce or move from city to city all the time usually don't notice the way life is always changing on you until they are almost grown. You are going to see a lot of stuff changing before things settle down into a more predictable, normal pattern.

Some of the changes you will encounter are big ones. You might have to move, be it down the block or across the country. You may have to change schools. You might have a whole new family structure complete with new and interesting people who you don't even know yet. These are all big things, but none of them is by definition a bad thing. Change is not a bad thing. It is a way of life.

Change does tend to include a period of chaos and adjustment before we can accept the new version of daily life. These big things shifting around you may not be easily worked into your familiar way of life. You are going to have to accept change as inevitable if you are going to live in this world anyway, so you might as well start here and now.

Everybody needs things to anchor them to their world. You, too. Going through big changes is easier if we can carry some familiar things with us—a best friend, a favorite quilt, a picture that we hang up on the wall the minute we move into a new bedroom. Music that you like helps, too. It can go anywhere with you. Change is easier if you find a way to take a bit of the old familiar stuff with you when you move into the new, unfamiliar places. But it's also easier if you don't try to keep everything the same in a situation where to do so is impossible. You'll have some sorting out to do. You'll be learning to keep what you can and to be hopeful that the things you have not been able to keep will soon feel less important to you than the new things you are getting into.

- When people get divorced, the life-style of everyone in the family changes; accept this and you are on the way.

- Change in itself is not bad. It's up to you to work with it rather than to work against it. (You can't win that one.)

- Attitude is key. If you look at the world through your desire for everything to stay the same, you will not be a happy camper.

I went to camp for the summer, and when I came back we had moved to a different city, one where we had lived before. So I moved into my mom's house and then two weeks later went to my dad's. I switched houses every two weeks. It was very difficult. I can't say that I regret doing it, though, because I think in a lot of divorces the children usually stay with the mother and don't see their father enough and lose contact with the father, and I think that it's very important to keep contact with both parents. That's something that I got from that and I'm really glad that I did that.

TRICIA, Age 17

It was kind of funny because one day my dad was there and the next day I was going weekends to his house. There had been certain fights and incidents. I remember that at Thanksgiving they had had a big blowout and they were trying to work it back together, but that didn't work out. I'm not sure really when they got separated. I remember them getting separated and then on weekends I was going to my dad's. There were certain things where the tension was high. I remember one time when I wanted to do something with my father and I asked him and he got really angry, so my mom went outside and did it. But my mom wasn't exactly the football playing type so she couldn't throw the football. Tensions were real high. I remember that. And I remember like from what I gather one of the last things was that my father said, "You're the oldest one now, you're the guy, and you've got to take care of the house and watch out." I was eight years old. And from what I gather my teacher asked my mom what had been going on because my attitude changed dramatically. I didn't really worry about school. I worried about what was going to happen to my mom.

TIM, Age 22

15

Don't Be Afraid to Tell Your Parents How You Feel

Truth is the only safe ground to stand upon.
—Elizabeth Cady Stanton

It is never a good idea to bottle stuff up inside you. Whether you believe it or not, it will come out in one way or another. If you are not honest with yourself or with the people whom you are closest to, it will affect your relationships with them and make you feel horrible in the end.

Sure, this is really easy to say here and for you to nod your head and skip on to the more exciting parts, but that's avoiding thinking about what you really want to say. There is a lot of stuff happening to you; you are probably feeling quite strongly about what is going on around you, and you should be able to talk about it with the people who are a part of it and/or the people who can listen and try to understand.

The hard part is figuring out exactly what you need to say and how to say it and, sometimes, to whom to say it.

61

Sometimes it is kind of obvious; you don't like it when your mom cuts your dad down. You tell your mom that you don't like it when she says horrible things about your father. Simple.

Other times you might be feeling vaguely uncomfortable about something. Often people can't explain exactly what's bothering them. This is another hard part, figuring out how you're feeling. Honesty with yourself rarely comes easily. The things that you think you *ought* to feel may not correspond as neatly as you'd like with the emotions that you are actually feeling. This is annoying at best and torturous at worst. Talking about it with one or both of your parents, explaining your confusion, disillusionment, anger, happiness, rapture, or whatever, may help you figure it out for yourself. Putting things into words at the right time to the right person isn't only an act of communication—it can help you explain things to yourself at the same time.

It's great if you want to tell your parents how you feel when you are feeling good (even though they may be shocked to hear from one of their kids when he or she has no immediate complaints!). You will have a more intense personal relationship with your parents. This usually happens because you are one-on-one with them a lot; it's one of the side effects of not seeing them together as a parental unit anymore. This closeness can be really nice, and it is great when you can tell them that you feel especially comfortable and good with them. Nothing floats a parent's boat more than hearing from you that you care and that you love them. Sincerity is mandatory when dealing with that stuff. Tell them how you feel, not how you wish you felt or how you think they want you to feel. Lying about stuff like that is the opposite of being open to working on your relationship. It will make you feel worse than if you hadn't said anything at all.

You can't be forced into telling someone how you feel. It is a matter of trust and assorted other stuff. They may come to you and be ready for a serious talk at a time when you really don't feel like chatting about your innermost feelings. Ask for a postponement. Make sure that you're having a deep talk when and because you want to, not just because it is what they want to do. But be up-front about it. If now is not a good time, explain that you'd like to talk later. Don't just tell them to bug off. If you're having a bad day, say so. If they seem to be copping an attitude you don't want to deal with, say so—politely.

You may soon find you're caught in a telling-them-how-you-feel frenzy. If you don't want to tell them how you feel, let them know that you're not up to it. It's kind of a trap. But at least you're being honest, right?

- You may be able to help yourself figure out how you feel or what is bothering you by talking about it even when it isn't quite clear in your own mind.

- Remember to tell them about the good stuff, too. They love that and you will feel great about it.

- Truth is a good thing. You're just hurting yourself by lying to them. It's worse for you than not saying anything in the first place.

My dad just like moved out and was instantly living with another lady. I just talked to him about this recently. He knows that it's really different now. I told him, "That's because you made this decision to move out. I'm not judging you on that, but you also moved right in with this woman. But this is a time when your relationship is going to be strained with your kids and you just chose somebody else because of your own

*needs and you didn't think about it." And I think that he kind
of realized it, but what can you say?*

ERICA, Age 19

*With my mom there've definitely been times when I've said to
her, "You know, will you just not say anything, can I just tell
you? And then we can talk about it later, but right now can
you just not say anything?" And she will. She's really great
about it. I'm lucky that way. . . . I think in a lot of ways what
I thought was, you know, my dad dumped all of this pain on
me and I couldn't give any of it back. Not that I wanted to
hurt him, but that I wanted to get rid of it. I couldn't get rid
of it by saying "Dad, take it back, I don't want it." So I had
to dispose of it in other ways. The laughter is one of the most
important things to me. The other day I was in the car with
my mom and we were just hysterically laughing over nothing
and I looked at her and I said, "Mom, I'm so glad we're both
so healthy right now, that we can do this. And I'm so glad that
we've both come so far."*

PAM, Age 19

16

Don't Let Your Parents' Divorce Become Your Whole Life

It has begun to occur to me that life is a stage I'm going through.

—ELLEN GOODMAN

Things at home are not how you'd like them to be. Okay. They are also not what you are used to or what you feel like you understand and can deal with. The reorganization of something you probably hadn't expected would ever be reorganized, namely your family, is indeed a big deal. But it's not the only deal.

Something to keep in mind is that there are lots of other things going on in your life at the same time, just as there were before the divorce. You are in an important stage of your growth as a human being, as people are likely to be reminding you, and growth is never a smooth process under any conditions. It's also unstoppable. You can't put it on hold while you immerse yourself in your parents' problems.

Many times people find out too late that they have been neglecting their friends, or that they didn't work as hard as they could have at school, or that they forgot to put in their application for the perfect summer job. They were distracted by their parents' divorce and didn't pay enough attention to the other things that were important in their own lives.

You need to take care of your own life and let your parents work things out for themselves as much as possible. It's not healthy to let their divorce dominate your life 24 hours a day, while things that are important to you slip through the cracks.

Sure, you want to know what's going on, and you have to see to it that you are not left in the dust of their divorce. You probably have new burdens and responsibilities connected with your home life, too, and plenty of emotional fallout from the whole situation. But check out all the other things going on in and around your life that are important to you—and do it frequently. How are they doing?

Whatever is going on in your parents' divorce, even if it is publicly messy and embarrassing, is something that they, not you, have brought about. You should not have to feel that everyone is looking at you now as just a part of that big mess (they're not, believe me), rather than as the bright, competent, cute human being you have always been.

At this point, for most of us, our self-image is very much tied to our image of our family. It's hard to feel that old family pride when your parents have become wild people you barely recognize. But they are not you. You are you. You don't need to hide out at home or devote yourself to making everything there better (or devote yourself to making it look as if it is better). You will be doing the greater good, for yourself, for your parents, and for the rest of your family, if you look at what needs to be taken care of in your own life and get on with it.

This is not a science fiction movie in which the divorce comes out of the sky and sucks the life and hobbies out of innocent children all over the world, thereby making them dull, lifeless legal dictionaries with a better understanding of local custody laws than of their own class schedules or week-end plans. This is your life. You have to see to it that you live it and don't just sit there and watch your parents' lives happen.

- You can take care of business and be on top of the divorce at the same time.

- You are the only person who can direct your own life in the way it ought to be going right now. Don't neglect it.

- The divorce in your family is a circumstance, not a life-time label. Devote yourself to nurturing your true identity, not your temporary role as a child of divorce.

This all happened in the eighties. Every TV show you saw, the couples were married. Being not in a family like that, I felt kind of left out, but my mom, like I said, she was my best friend, and because she got along so well with me, she was like another buddy to my friends, so we had a great time. Sometimes my dad, when we'd see him on the weekends, he told us we could bring friends with us. So I always brought a friend with me. So they still saw my parents. I guess they didn't think it was strange, because they didn't see my dad in my house anyway, and seeing them separately was still the same. My parents didn't change as people. And I didn't change. I was still the same person and my friends still accepted me. I was the one feeling weird. I got over it quickly. I told myself, it's a part of life. It happens. Actually, I'm happier this way. When they told me they were getting back together, I was sort of disappointed.

I really didn't want it. It's better that they never did get back together.

LISA, Age 19

Actually, I've had people admire me. Because even though my mother was divorced, she did more for me than some people with two parents. So it was like, "Wow, let's go to Ronnie's house." I had more people behind me than saying, "Well, don't you feel awkward because you don't have two parents?" There was like a few times when I felt like I wanted to know my father, and after that I just felt normal. I felt more like I had more freedom than anyone else, actually. She trusted me more. She didn't have that man there telling her, "Look, don't let her go out with guys 'til she's this age." My mother was like this: You do this and you do it this way and everything will be fine. She never gave me a curfew and yet I was home by twelve. She never told me that I couldn't talk to guys on the phone, but yet I didn't take advantage of it. She didn't tell me not to date guys. I was free but I didn't take advantage of it. It's to the point where even if I do something a teensy bit wrong, like maybe come home an hour late, it's like I feel bad. So I have myself on a set schedule. And I have goals, that if I don't achieve them, then I feel bad. I don't care what anybody else says, I will feel bad.

RONNIE, Age 22

Ronnie's mother has been married three times. Her first husband is the father of Ronnie, 22, and her older sister. He and her mother separated when Ronnie was three years old. Ronnie, her mother, and her sister moved in with Ronnie's grandparents.

"My father came down one time to visit us and he stole us. I was three and my sister was five," she says. "He took us back to his town and my grandparents came and got us. They said we were standing in front of the door with just diapers on. I think my sister had just some shorts on or something, and they grabbed us. That was when my mother went ahead and got divorced and got a restraining order against him. He couldn't see us.

"Instead of making an effort to call or something like that, he never really had any dealings with us after that. He never called us. I think the next time that I talked to him was probably when I turned nine and the next time after that was recently."

Ronnie's mother had remarried when Ronnie first decided to get in touch with her father again. She says, "I missed my father and I wanted to know about my father. . . . I called his family and they gave me his number. . . . I didn't see him when I was nine, I just spoke to him. I saw him the second time when I was nineteen. I found him again. I had gotten sick. I had gotten lupus when I was seventeen. We talked with him then because my mom wanted his help with money. Doctors' visits were like two hundred dollars, and I had to go twice a week when it first started. And he totally cut her off. He said that it was because of the way she lived that I had gotten sick, and, you know, a lot of stuff. I still didn't cut him totally out. I said I'm going to give him another chance. I found him and we got together. We drove to see his family, and after I talked to him and figured out he really had nothing to say, nothing to say that was important, and he really couldn't give a good excuse for leaving me almost at death with no help, with my mom by herself, after that I haven't talked to him since then. And I don't want to talk to him.

"My mother has always worked. She's always been the one that's been like the mother and the father. I can remember a few times between then and now when she's worked two jobs just to make sure me and my sister were okay. We never suffered. *She* might have suffered, but we never suffered. She tried to make my life as normal as possible. Like if I had a friend that had two parents and they had something, she would try to do whatever they could do, but only by herself. She married my next father, which is whom I call my father, he— they—were married probably for like the core of my life, because it was from the time I was little until teenage years. He was pretty good with us when we were little. I had run-ins with him when I started into my teenage years, because he was a little strict on going out, curfews, which was probably the best thing for me, but at that time I was upset about it. Now, me and him, we're like best friends. He's the one who helped me get back into school, who encouraged me to do it. . . . He did the stuff with us that I think my real father should have done. He took us on vacations and every time I saw him he was always working to help keep a roof over our heads.

"As far as my mom goes, though, they didn't hit it off too well. He cheated on her and they used to always fight and argue. They never did it around us, but I was nosy and I would listen. She basically kept him for probably five more years than she should have, probably just because she wanted us to have a father. After they separated he still did things for us. He wasn't our biological father, but he still took us out, tried to pick us up on weekends. . . . I had a couple of problems because he would whine about my mother and how he wanted her back and she didn't want him anymore, but they finally got a divorce and I still spent time with him. And he finally met up with someone else, who he's now married to. And she's really wonderful. Now he's really happy.

"My mom is, well, okay. After she got their divorce, she married a new man. He's the one I live with now, with Mom, him, and my sister. And I'd say that he's pretty abusive. In the beginning it was everything was sweet. And then there was a time when my mom lost her job and he just totally—it was like, 'I'm the one who brings home all the money, I'm the controller.' And he started beating on her. It was almost a year she didn't have a job. My sister and I kept telling her, 'Let's leave, we will work.' I dropped out of college and came home. We were like, 'We'll work and we'll pay for another place. Why don't we move together and then you can find a place?'

"She didn't want to leave him. So we left her. That was an experience. We left and we tried to get our own place, and my sister ended up getting pregnant and she lost her job and then it was just me taking care of the place and I couldn't afford it. My grandparents had to pay our last rent for us and we had to move in with our grandparents. We tried to move out again and we couldn't afford it. Then we ended up living with other people. My sister started living with other relatives and I started living with an ex-girlfriend of one of my uncles.

"I ended up staying with her and getting on my feet, getting a job, getting a car, saving money. My sister on the other hand didn't have a job for like three years. She just got a job last year. My mother got a job. It wasn't good, but it was okay. Then she wanted to leave him. So we all got together, we moved in together and we left him.

"It was about six months they weren't seeing each other and somehow he wheedled his way back in. I don't know how he did that. . . . We didn't want to move back in together. So they got together, they started to buy a house together. This is the house we're living in now. He hasn't done anything abusive, I'd say—well, actually, last summer, just before I started school, he tried something and I called the police on him. And they put him in jail overnight. But that's the only thing he's done probably in the last year and a half now. I think for the most part it's kind of sad. I'm glad she's with him only for company, but if I could find someone else to be with her I'd probably choose someone else.

"I try to do— I don't get any money from her for school and supplies, I do all that on my own so she doesn't have extra bills or anything. But sometimes I have to act as the mother and give her money, because she's totally broke. I'm so used to it. It's a job for me.

"I'm afraid of the time when I want to move out. I'm going

to feel guilty. But I'm not going to move too far, just because I don't want to leave my mother. She can call me whenever she needs something. I'd give up my last dime for her. She did it for me.

"I've talked to her about how I feel about them being together, but it doesn't get me anywhere. We've done this for years. They've been with each other for almost eight or nine years now. He has his good points. He's nice at times, but at the same time . . . She loves him. . . . She's always told me if they didn't last she'd never get married again, but she said that about the second one, so . . . I don't know.

"Even though she's married all these men or whatever, I usually don't pay attention to that. I usually just pay attention to how happy she is. And all the hard work she's done to raise my sister and me by herself. I always say 'by herself' because they've come in and out and she's always been there. . . .

"My grandparents are really religious. They're into this thing where unless your spouse dies you're still married to him. So they will just rip your parents to shreds in your face. If they say something, they usually don't come out and say things to me, they say them to my sister because she takes it, but if they do, I'm like, 'That's my business,' or 'Why are you even bringing that up?' I even tell them, 'Well, you're supposed to be a man of God, why are you talking about something like that?' That really burns them up, when you talk about religion. They're just supposed to care and help. They're not supposed to talk about you behind your back, which they do all the time. . . .

"When my sister got pregnant, I was the one that took care of her because the father was a bum, basically. He wasn't there. I was the one that made sure she had someone there with her the weekend she went into labor to have the baby. I was the one there with her in the hospital. I wasn't in the labor room with her, it was him. But when the whole family turned against her because she was pregnant and not married, everybody called her everything in the book. Even when the baby was there they were talking about, 'This isn't my grandson, this isn't my great-grandson. I don't know who this is.' And I was the one sticking up for her. I even like wouldn't go around my family for a while because they really tore her to pieces. And I'm sensitive, but when it comes to comments like that, I know how to come back with it. I get real angry. But she will cry. She will close herself up, she will not say anything, she will hold it in, and then one day she might just burst open. But I helped her a lot through that. I watched her go through having a really decent job to having nothing. To losing her car, losing her place to live, losing half the stuff she owned, and then I watched her rebuild herself again. It took a while. She rebuilt herself back probably this summer. She managed to get a job, a car, and go back to school, within four months. Which is really good.

"From the time that she lost everything until then, I was the one supporting her. If she needed money, if she needed a ride somewhere, I was the one doing it. Even though I'd hear from people, 'Why are you doing that? She's never going to get back on her feet.' I listened to that for three years. 'You need to talk to her. She's never going to change. She's going

to be living off people, she'll be on welfare for the rest of her
life. She's not gonna raise her child right.' I mean, everything.
And I'd always tell them, 'Look, don't worry about it, I'll talk
to her.' It got to the point where I was fed up myself, but I
never turned my back on her. Because I love her. Because I
know if you help someone enough they will change. I just
believe that. I've seen it happen so many times. And I mean
even my mother almost washed her hands of her. She was just
like, 'I can't take this. I just can't take this. She's lazy.' She
wouldn't clean. You're home, you have no job, you clean. You
clean, you cook, whatever. She wouldn't do any of that. She
was depressed. That's one of the reasons I didn't leave her. It
wasn't like she was lazy, she had no self-esteem. . . . She did
good, though. She showed some people. I don't know what
turned her around. I kept telling her that she has the qualities
to get a good job. She's really good with computers and if
you know computers you can probably get just about any job.
I kept telling her, 'Look, just go on and get something and if
you don't like it, it will give you some money until you find
something better.' And she went out on an interview that she
found in the paper and it was a good job and she got it. And
it was great. She's really good at it.

"She hated my real father. When I called him she didn't
want to talk to him. . . . My second father, the one that we
call our father, they're really close. They go out probably more
than me and him go out. When she was down he also sup-
ported her. He's decent. He kept telling her about jobs, trying
to help her get applications. Just helped her out. Picked her
up, did things with her to try to make her feel better about
herself. And it worked.

"My mother's husband now. . . . I don't care how much my mother loves him. If he tries to come between her and us, he'll have to go. She's always told him, 'My kids come first.' And he used to complain about it, argue about it. And she would tell him, 'I don't care if they're fifty years old, they will come before you.' After that one time I left I promised her I'd never do it again. I felt so bad when I did that. I didn't feel bad when I did it. It was afterward when I looked at everything and I thought, you know, I could have handled it differently.

"Sometimes I wish I had less responsibility. I feel like I can't have my own life until I feel like they're okay. I mean, I have my own life, but it's so on a schedule. I can't say, 'Well, I think after this class I'm going to go hang over so-and-so's house.' That's what I miss. I have a boyfriend. And it's kind of hard for me to really put myself into a relationship with him, because I have so many things to do at home and at school. So I have to prioritize everything now. And how long is my boyfriend going to be around compared to my degree? So school comes first, my homework and everything, and I guess my home and my boyfriend are on the same level. . . .

"I always wondered if she would have stayed with maybe her second husband, and I say him because he's maybe the most stable one of all of them, would I have had more, would I have to work so hard to get stuff now, would I have stayed in the first school I was in, would I have had a degree already? If he was there, he would have been hell-bent on keeping me in school until I got that degree instead of me jumping from school to school like I had to do. And taking breaks. And not having enough money to go back. He would have made it so

I'd have stayed, I know that much. . . . I probably would have had a lot of things I don't have now. But, in fact, I'm doing all right. I really can't complain. I have some problems, but who doesn't have problems?

"The first semester I came back to school I had almost a full-time job. It was about twenty-five or thirty hours, but I only had four classes. I couldn't keep the job and be in school. So I passed the job on to my mother. Now I make little gift baskets on the side. I sell them to her friends. I have some people that buy them every holiday for fifteen or twenty dollars. It's just little odd jobs. That's the only thing I can do right now because I do not want to jeopardize my grades this semester. I want to get better grades than I did last, and the only way I can do that is if I have more time to do homework. I got some money back from some of the loans, from financial aid, from tax returns, and some money from an accident. That will carry me over to the summer and I plan on working full-time during the summer. You have to plan it out to work right, but I refuse to run out of money and I don't want to ask anybody either."

17

Have Some Personal Space Where You Can Get Away

Humankind cannot bear very much reality.

—T.S. ELIOT

Everyone needs time to themselves. This time alone, or at least separate, can be very important. It tends to be even more important when your life is changing in strange ways. Some people need to get away more than others, but just about everyone needs an occasional break just to help sort things out. There's nothing wrong with wanting to be alone sometimes. It only becomes a problem if you isolate yourself all the time or if you are alienating the people you care for.

When your whole life changes dramatically, when your family is doing strange things that you don't necessarily understand, and when your home doesn't feel so homey anymore, you will probably need a place where you can get out from the middle of it all and just think, just relax, or just do nothing—a place or circumstance where you are not smack in the middle of other people's messes, moods, fits, catastrophes, or manias.

Your room could be such a place, but a lot of people find that because it is a part of the house where distressing things are happening, it doesn't really work for them. Maybe you have a coffee shop that you like to sit in. You may like going to the library and hanging out in the fiction section. You could ride your bike in the park or drive around listening to loud music. You should take whatever route works, as long as it is not damaging to you in other ways. A little bit of escapism never hurt anyone.

You don't need to cut yourself off from your home; in fact, that is not the point at all. There is a big difference between running away from your problems and taking a break from them. Running away doesn't help anyone, including you. Taking a break is necessary.

Chances are that you are having more trouble with what's going on in your own head than with whatever is actually going on at home anyway, and everyone knows that you can't get away from yourself. You will always be with yourself, so you need to straighten that stuff out. Besides, running away from stuff isn't relaxing—it's actually more stressful.

It is possible to attain personal space right in the comfort of your own home. You can listen to your favorite song loudly (headphones are a good idea), you can write, or read, or compose, or paint. You can exercise. It's certainly good for a time-out and you can take out all those ugly frustrations at the same time that you get all fit and healthy. Any hobby where you can lose yourself briefly, any kind of activity that helps you relax and be happy, is a good idea. You can cook or clean or stare at the ceiling. What works for you may not be what works for other people. Escapism is a personal thing. You have to figure out what works for you and not push yourself to do the things that don't, even if someone else is telling you they'd be good for you.

Sometimes people don't understand the need for space and time off. Maybe they just don't understand why you like to sit in dark coffee shops. You should point out to these people that they like to sit and read the paper without interruption, that they like to go jogging at six in the morning. Point out to them that they also need time and space and that there is nothing wrong with coffee shops or Jethro Tull. If your need for personal space is really disturbing them you can try to work out some kind of understanding where you still get the time you need. It is never good to alienate the people you care about in the name of sorting stuff out.

- Everyone needs space. Find something that helps and stick with it for as long as you want.

- Make sure that it is not something damaging. Please.

- You can get the time you need without pushing other people away too much.

I guess I can't change my parents. If I could do things differently, I guess I'd talk more. Everything was about what was happening to my mother, her, her, her, her. I think I'd be louder, more assertive. I didn't have much time to pay attention to myself. I was always busy with my sister, my cousin. Except when we went to my grandmother's. Time stood still there. I could relax.

MARIANNE, Age 25

When I was 14, I left home for a year to live with my cousins in California, a family. And that, I think, gave me a huge break and really saved me in a way. I never missed my parents, I never missed my home. I was thrilled to be out of there. It was just very free. So I had a year off. My cousins just needed somebody to take care of their kid after school. She was five. I liked it. I felt like a part of a family and I have a lot of family out there, and they're all in a little town sort of close together so I could ride my bike anywhere and visit family, which meant a lot to me. That particular living situation wasn't free from tension, really, it was very, very tense and stressful. I think they had marital problems. But still, just to be out of the other was such a giant relief. And for the first time to feel like I belonged to a family. It felt like nothing else. I took care of myself better there.

LAURA, Age 22

18

Stay Active: Don't Hibernate

The hardest thing to believe when you're young is that people will fight to stay in a rut, but not to get out of it.

—Ellen Glasgow

Sitting at home when home is at least temporarily the center of the problems that are messing with your mind is probably not a good idea. Avoiding social opportunities in favor of curling up in the dim light of your bedroom gives you a lot of time to go over things in your own head. This can be useful. It can also be really horrible, especially when you end up going round and round over the same troubling turf. It's a good way to end up blowing things out of proportion and to stress about things over which you have no control.

Sometimes things that seem easy turn out to be a kind of trap. If you lie in bed freezing and thinking you are just too lazy to get up and get another blanket, that it would take more effort than it's worth, you will probably be cold and sleepless the entire night. But if you make the effort to get out of bed for a minute and get a nice, warm comforter, you can change your atmosphere entirely and be on your way to pleasant dreams immediately.

A little effort can go a long way. You can sit home alone in your room or take action to get yourself out among people. You don't have to try anything too new or intimidating. It's perfectly okay to go hang out at a friend's house or ask someone to meet you for tacos. Just do *something*.

Be good to yourself. Stay busy. You will have plenty of time to think things through while you are making your way to the movie/bowling alley/yearbook meeting/soccer practice. And the fresh air will do you good.

- Get out of your room. A change of pace and atmosphere can point you toward a change of perspective. Things may not look so bad to you after all.

- You do *not* need more time to think. In fact, you probably need less time.

- Guaranteed: There are more possibilities for happiness out in the world than there are in your room.

A lot of people seem to think that kids with divorced parents have a particularly difficult time getting involved in activities and maintaining personal relationships. A group of people in a psychology class I was taking explained in great theoretical detail why children of divorce stay home and sulk. I have not found this to be the case. Personally, I didn't want to hang around the house. It was kind of an escapist tactic at first, but as I got more involved in my chosen activities and closer with my friends, my life ceased to revolve around things happening at home, including The Divorce. I worked really hard at my school yearbook as a photographer and discovered that I love photography. I eventually became photo editor (which, by the way, can do wonders for that ravaged self-esteem people keep talking about). I also worked as a technician in the school theater, and that led to a job building sets at a professional stage in town. The friends who shared these activities with me were like a family to me. When I think about going home now, I think of them at least as often as I do of my "real" family.

NORA, Age 20

I focused on art. If I didn't have art to turn to, I'd be lost. Bicycling, walking for a couple of hours, you can clear your mind of everything. There is a lot of anger. I used to go to deep relaxation sessions with a therapist. At the end of the sessions when I was very relaxed I would just cry. And I realized it was because of all the feelings I was keeping down inside of me.

TARA, Age 23

19

Develop Your Sense of Timing for Discussing Those "Deep Subjects" with Your Parents

Parents are not interested in justice. They are interested in quiet.

—BILL COSBY

Timing is of the essence. You have to be extremely careful around people who are having a difficult time emotionally. They can be like time bombs. It is not good to light fires under explosives and it is not good to insist on getting into heavy stuff with your parents at the wrong time.

Nobody knows your parents' moods better than you do. Chances are you have been playing off them, evaluating them, evading them, and/or dealing with them for quite some time now. This is not necessarily manipulation; it is just sensitivity, good judgment, and self-preservation on your part to know what you can expect when you talk to your folks.

If you want to talk to your mother about how you're feeling about the divorce, how things are going, you want to select the time wisely. Under the heading "Caution," you may want to consider whether she has had a particularly rough day, or just spent the day in court with your father (Danger!). If you know that she is going through some serious negative stuff with your dad at the time, keep in mind that people tend not to be very diplomatic when they are hurt.

If you see that it is a bad time to discuss things, wait. Learn patience. If it can wait until a "good" time, well then, let it. If you absolutely need to talk right now, proceed with caution. One of the many ways in which you could start a poorly timed conversation without unwarranted bitterness could go something like this: "Mom, I know that this is a bad time, but I really would like to talk to you about ..." Obvious? Well, yeah. But it is better than, "So, Mom, are you still ticked about this divorce thing?" It is really easy to start off on the wrong foot.

You are probably not used to choosing your words one by one when talking to your parents. Diplomacy is one of those things that marks the line between being a kid and being an adult. Your family's divorce is doing a lot to kick you right over that line, so you may as well add a useful skill like diplomacy to your knapsack while you're at it.

In case this hasn't been beaten into the ground yet, your folks are having a rough time. Having a rough time does not excuse poor behavior, but it will be better for you if you learn how to avoid angering them unnecessarily. One thing that will help is if you can make a habit of talking to your parent or parents, rather than talking to them only when you are all hot and bothered. That way when they see you coming they won't think, "Oh no, here comes another difficult discussion."

You may want to talk about things going on in your life

other than the divorce and its accompanying issues (stranger things have happened). Timing is just as important here as it is in a divorce discussion. Before you instigate a talk about your goals in life, or your problems at school, or the color of the grass on Mars, or whatever, check out the territory and the weather around your mom or dad.

Divorcing parents and divorced parents have a tendency to be hypersensitive about lots of things. They are in the middle of getting rid of a significant portion of their family. They are trying to build a new life while doing without a very important part of their old one, and you are what they have left to work with. You have also been privy to a big, unpleasant episode in the adult world. They may feel embarrassed about that. And you are probably feeling a lot older than they think. If you are going to talk adult talk, you are also going to have to choose adult moments. You should know that it is a bad idea to talk to your dad about choosing colleges when he is trying to balance his checkbook.

It's important for you to find a way to have good, productive, helpful discussions with your parents. Be wise. Be patient. Take a measure of which way the wind is blowing before you plunge in and start yakking.

- If you know that it is a bad time to talk and it can wait: Let it wait.

- Understand that timing can be the difference between a heart-to-heart talk and a screaming match. Sure, this isn't really optimal, but that's the way it is.

- If it can't wait, choose your words with care. You don't want to make this any worse than it has to be. In fact, choose your words with care anyway.

- Never talk to them when they're in the bathroom. They hate that.

If I get into an argument with my mom at the wrong time I can still bug her out. I feel like I give her guilt trips when I don't mean to. I would have thought I was right and I didn't realize that what I was saying was giving her a guilt trip. She's cool now, I guess, but she's still kind of fragile.

CHARLIE, Age 21

My dad and I just have had this relationship since I was about 13 or so, when I spent my tenth grade year without him speaking to me for the entire year. That's just how it goes and that's how I react to him, so we have very hard times letting each other know we love each other. It's a really unfortunate relationship. We know we love each other, but it's like my personality really bothers him. He's a very religious person and he's always concerned for my spiritual welfare, but he and my mom talk about it and she tries to be the mediator. We even had a meeting after my uncle's funeral in March, we set up a meeting at my mom's for the three of us and she was going to be like the referee and he was going to tell me everything. I hadn't talked to him since I'd left my husband in June, so he just wanted to get it out on the table. He didn't really want a dialogue. He wanted to tell me what he thought. I was so scared. I just hate conflict of any kind. My mom was going to be there, and on the way to her house she was saying well, "What would you tell him? You need to talk, you need to tell him what you think." So I was like all mad and I was saying all this stuff and she said, "You should just tell him that, and I'll be there."

JILL, Age 28

20

Try Not to Worry About Things You Can't Control

To fear is one thing. To let fear grab you by the tail and swing you around is another.

—KATHERINE PATERSON

Worrying about things you can't realistically control is a favorite pastime for many people. We worry about the government, about international issues, about the environment, about life on other planets, about starving children in obscure parts of the world. These are but a few examples that come to mind when one thinks of senseless worrying.

Civic action is good and all, but you can't feed every baby or care for every sick person out there. You probably know this, and if you still feel inclined to make the world a better place you can do some volunteer work or get involved with an organization or club and work on a chosen corner of the whole. This is macroworrying being fixed by microwork. You worry about a big picture and try to do your part to fix a piece of it.

Same goes for home and family. You can't fix everything. And it's just self-destructive to stress out over recognition of that fact. You have to do what you can with what you've got and leave the rest alone.

If you can't make your mother love your dad there is no use in worrying about it. Your energy is better spent dealing with things as they are rather than thinking about how you wish they were.

As small children, we tend to look up to the tall people around us as the ones who know what they are doing and who know what is going on. They did all of the worrying for us when we were little. They knew the bus schedule, they made the lunches and helped with homework.

As long as the problems were simple, so were the solutions. When the issues got tougher, as in divorce, their experience failed them. They would not have been married if they had intended from the start to get divorced, so naturally they are a bit unprepared and bumbling about the whole deal. Rest assured that they are probably worrying enough for both of you and that they, too, feel out of control and adrift on the currents of uncharted waters.

It's really too bad that you can't just flip a switch in your head that would turn off the "worry" function so you could get some sleep. Worry, fear, and anxiety are all intensely unpleasant feelings. They were made to be that way. If we liked feeling afraid and anxious we would do nothing to avoid those feelings. Indeed, we would pursue anxiety, put it on a leash, take it home, and ask if we could keep it.

Alas, we just don't have a quick remedy for senseless worrying. Reading this chapter will by no means make you nod your head and say, "So, that's how it is. I'll just stop worrying now and everything will be fine." Nope. Sorry. It's not quite that easy. Let's just hope that it has given you something to think about and shown you a glimmer of light at the end of the tunnel. Yes, there are things that are out of your control. Welcome to the human race. Relax and enjoy the ride.

- Everyone is clueless. If you're worried about that, stop it. If nothing else, the confusing experiences you are having now will make you significantly less clueless in the future.

- Learn how to tell when you can't fix something. Then leave it alone.

- People who always have control over absolutely everything either don't exist or aren't really having any fun.

I didn't always have people to talk to. I turned to drawing, things about nature. I was kind of eccentric when I was younger. I was really into dressing up in costumes and doing fairly imaginative things. I guess in some ways it helped me. I had a little ventriloquist's dummy. It was Groucho Marx. It was funny because it was in a three-piece suit and it had a cigar. I used to walk around talking to it and stuff. It was almost like I was relating with my dad in some ways and was talking to him. It was kind of weird. My life is pretty good now. But it's very interesting to look back on the way things can be. And I can relate to a lot of people now, how they must feel not to be able to look up to somebody. It's really terrible. Going to an inner city school last year made me realize I hadn't gone through nearly as much as some of the people. I feel really lucky just to be in school and just to be able to feed my mind. I do a lot of sins, but I feel that I'm a very spiritually headed

*person. I feel that when I'm older I'm going to find that spiritu-
ality in me.*

JOSH, Age 18

*Because I didn't drive, I couldn't go to church and talk to a
priest. But just recently I've started to do that. Before, too, I
didn't want to talk to anyone because I didn't want them thinking my mom was a bad mom. Because she didn't really do
anything. It's just what happened. So I cried a lot. Now that I
can talk to a priest, I don't do it very often, but whenever our
financial problems get so bad that we think we might be evicted
or something, I run to church and I sit there and something
always comes up and it helps us. There's always a guardian
angel.*

LISA, Age 19

21

Holidays Will Be Strange

Holidays
Have no pity.

—Eugenio Montale

Holidays are going to be kind of odd for quite some time, possibly for years and years. It might be a good kind of odd, though. Once you get used to whatever your personal situation is, you may feel free to revel in the discomfort of others. That is, it isn't just us kids of divorce who have trouble with holidays.

Especially at holiday times, the media bombard us with frequent, merciless, and inaccurate images of "happy," together, normal families. The media lie. The fact of the matter is that just about every family has some glitch that makes it less than "normal." Yours just has a label affixed to it that reads, d-i-v-o-r-c-e.

You are going to feel odd running from Mom's house to Dad's for two Thanksgiving dinners; you may feel strange alternating holidays with each of them. What's not to feel strange about there?

Every custody arrangement seems to account for holidays in a different way, depending largely on what the parents are able to agree on. It can be a real bone of contention. Festival times are accompanied by all kinds of psychological pressures, as you probably know, and you really don't need the added stress of dealing with which parent you ought to be with. It's usually best when families come up with a regular way of dealing with the holidays year round, rather than negotiating each holiday separately just before it arrives. At least one of the routine holiday anxieties can be minimized that way.

We are all brought up to think of holidays as times of family togetherness and love and peace and all kinds of cheese like that. Sure, it's nice one day a year or something, but when it is overdone, it runs the risk of getting downright sickening. Some kids have trouble with the holidays because of the memories that are brought back. It is kind of like facing the first day of school after your best friend has moved to another state. It is just hard to cope with the team when some of the players are missing.

The whole dynamic changes when your family splits. It may turn out that it's just you and your mother for New Year's. This would be a big change from the days when it was you, your parents, and a gang of their friends and other relatives. Some traditions will fall away, but this is not necessarily bad. It also presents an opportunity to start new family traditions to go along with your new family structure.

Another common complaint from kids with divorced parents concerns those times when everyone tries to get along and play family for the sake of the relatives. This rarely fails to get messy and painful for all concerned. It can make everyone much more unhappy to have one parent hanging around with his or her ex's family just for the sake of appearances. It can make things more tense than they need be, sadder than if that parent celebrated the holiday elsewhere and without you.

Reach an understanding with your parents on what you do and don't like about how they are working out the holidays. Sometimes, expressing your views can help resolve differences between the two of them. They probably both want what's best for you, so tell them.

- Holidays really can't help but be strange once a family structure has been radically altered. Get used to it and give the new arrangements a chance.

- If the holidays are working out in a way that is too stupid, stressful, or painful to be worth it, work with your parents to change things.

- Refuse to feel strange about your family. There is nothing odd about celebrating holidays with stepparents, a parent's boy or girlfriend, single parents, and/or extended family. Think of it this way: You are diverse in your relationships. This makes you special and sophisticated, not deprived.

Holidays are the worst. Thanksgiving is all right. But Christmastime— Last year I remember sitting on my dad's bed, just crying just because—like, he lived at my grandparents' house and he doesn't get along with my aunt. There's my grandmother's house and she lives there with my grandfather, and next door is my aunt, my dad's sister, and she has my cousin Barbara, who's like 11 or 12 now. And my grandmother takes care of Barbara a lot because both of her parents work, and my grandmother cooks for my aunt and her husband too a lot, and my dad just gets so angry. He says, "You know Grandma has enough problems and stuff and you bring your crap over here." He causes so much problems in the house. And every year for Christmas I went to my grandmother's house. The whole family did. And last year my dad said, "What are you doing for Christmas?" I said, "I'm going to Grandma's." And he just got really mad and said, "Well, I'm not going, I'm not going to that house." I'm like, "Dad, it's your family." "No," he said, "I'm going to Bobbie's house. Where are you going?" I said, "I want to go to Grandma's house and I want to be with you. And my ideal is for you to be there." And he's like, "Well, I'm your father and you should be with me for Christmas," and I'm, "Well, I'm going to go to Grandma's, but I'll go to Bobbie's house, too." And I told him this when we were out to dinner and he got so mad. He gave me a bunch of money, he threw me like twenty dollars and he was like, "Here, pay the bill, I'm leaving." And he just left me there. This was last year. I was 18 years old. Thank God we both drove there or I'd have been stuck there.

JEFF, Age 19

My mom was crying and I had to be there for her. I mean, you know, let her talk to me. It really hurt when I saw my mom crying. She was upset because she couldn't give me everything I wanted for Christmas. Ever since then I've hated Christmas. I guess when I have my children I'll learn to respect Christmas again.

ROB, Age 20

We alternate holidays. This year I had Christmas with my mother and spring break with my father and Thanksgiving with my father, and then like Memorial Day and Martin Luther King's birthday with my mom. They alternate it every year. It goes systematically. I think that's a good arrangement. It was written into their agreement.

TRICIA, Age 17

22

Your New Responsibilities May Be Good for You

I don't like work—no man does—but I like what is in the work—the chance to find yourself.

—JOSEPH CONRAD

Kids learn some of the most useful stuff when they least want to. Chances are that when your parents get divorced you are going to have more responsibilities. This tends to be the rule for most families. If Dad walked the dog while Mom made the coffee, there is a gap in the routine that needs to be filled when Mom moves out. A lot of people learn to cook when their parents split up. They start taking more responsibility for their own lives, too.

Self-sufficiency is the goal of the child of divorce. Kids learn quickly when they can't depend on much in the way of home stability. They learn how to get their homework done on their own, they learn how to shop for groceries, they learn to talk to auto mechanics. They learn how to sew on buttons, how to earn more money for themselves . . . The list goes on.

Practical little chores are not the only kinds of responsibility you are likely to learn about. Lots of people end up taking care of their parents or their brothers and sisters during this rough time, and that can help you grow as an individual. You could learn how to talk to your mother or father about serious matters and how to relate to other adults in a more mature and effective manner (including teachers, who can help you when your parents are temporarily out of order). You will undoubtedly learn a lot about human relationships and laundry. Laundry is a skill that a surprising number of people do not master before they leave home. You would be astonished at the things college students put into a standard washing machine and expect to get clean. You may not be a sorting wizard, but if you've been taking care of yourself for a while you will certainly know better than to put that silk shirt in hot water with bleach.

But back to the subject: Think of your new responsibilities as survival skills to take with you to that ever elusive "real world" that you are always being threatened with. If you pay attention, you may end up as self-reliant as the lost camper who manages to light a fire with only one wet match.

If you have to get a job to make your own spending money, good for you. Other people will be jealous of your opportunity and thrift. No, that's a lie. But you will have something to be proud of when telling stories to your kids about how hard life was for you: "When I was your age [insert hard luck story] . . ." That job will be the doorway to other jobs. Surprising though it may seem, there comes a time when it is almost too late to get a first job. No employer wants to talk to a 20-year-old with no paid experience at anything. Just think, you will have years of employment experience to list on your application for the job of your dreams. And meanwhile, you'll have some cash. Work is also a place to learn stuff that you would never have thought you'd need to know—not just job skills, but things about yourself. But that's another book entirely.

So, whatever your new responsibilities may be, they are probably good for you in some way. If nothing else, they are sure to build character—a veritable tower of character. If you're walking the dog or paying the bills, you will be such a good dog walker and bill payer by the time you leave home that you can give helpful hints to others and gain the respect and admiration of your peers.

Taking on a few adult responsibilities is good for you. You learn a lot about people when you have to fill their shoes for a while. You will gain some extra perspectives that are certain to be valuable for a long time to come.

- If you have to do something anyway, you might as well profit from it. Knowledge can be profit. Pay attention.

- Think about all the stuff that you know how to do now that you didn't know before.

- Surreptitious learning is sometimes the best kind. The most important stuff can sneak up on you when you least expect it, and it can come from the most unlikely sources.

- Always use fabric softener.

I cook, I clean, I do my own laundry. It does help me out. I've talked to some of my friends. You know, maybe their dad's a doctor and their mom stays home and does housework and they don't have to do a lot of cooking and cleaning and stuff, so they don't really know how. Plus, I live with my mom and I see her as a woman in the business world trying to make it.

She's making it well. Living with her as a divorced mother, I gain more respect for her. I don't know if it turned me into a feminist or anything, but seeing what she has to put up with in the business world, just talking to her and stuff, I learn things. I've had some English teachers in high school who were pretty male chauvinistic. I think I'm more conscious of that.

JEFF, AGE 19

My sister is not very emotional. She just shrugs things off, like, oh well. When I visited her I got really mad at my father and said how he hadn't visited in a while, how he's so irresponsible. And she just said, "Well, I'm not going to waste any time on that." And I just looked at her and said, "How can you be that way?" But she doesn't know as much stuff about him as I do, because I sheltered her. She's learning. She knows about his drug habits. But she's just really calm. And I think, why can't I be like her so I could concentrate on my work? I mean, she's a really private person. Nothing bothers her, she won't let it. She just keeps going. For her to grow up the way that she did, I think, maybe I did something good for her. She'll be going to college this September and she got into Stanford, Columbia, and Tulane. She's trying to decide where to go. She's going to look at the schools over spring break. She went to private school, we got her tested, and she got a full scholarship. She does really well. And I know I helped with that, and I feel good about it.

MARIANNE, AGE 25

23

Figure Out Ways to Make Moving Between Your Parents' Homes Comfortable

A house that does not have one worn, comfy chair in it is soulless.

—MAY SARTON

You probably didn't have a whole lot of influence on your particular custody/visitation arrangement. Whatever your parents and their lawyers worked out was the best compromise they could all agree on. Even if they did ask you how you felt about the whole thing, even if they let you help make the arrangements, it will probably feel pretty strange while you're all getting used to it.

Some people become accustomed to their new, more mobile way of life. It is even possible that some kids revel in their options, independence, flexibility, and ability to schedule three people's lives (Mom, Dad, and child) into a neat, legally responsible package. Still, it doesn't mean that it is always the most convenient or easiest thing in the world.

You might feel that you are caught in a twisted game of Ping-Pong, with you as the ball and your parents as players on opposing sides of the table. You get banged back and forth with some regularity, at their convenience, regardless of what you've got going. Perhaps they are a bit more sensitive and keep to a schedule that allows some flexibility for your ever-changing plans.

Most often, it seems that weekend visits with the nonresident parent are the rule, except when a lot of distance separates your folks. People spend every weekend, every other weekend, or one weekend a month with the "other" parent. How does this work out for you? Does running off to a different home totally screw up your plans? It may be that it will work out fine, that it will be pretty convenient for all that you want to do. There may be advantages to the time you spend at your nonresident parent's house—a bit of an escape from your everyday life. It may be that it is a royal pain, messing up everything you usually do, isolating you from your friends and activities. You have to make the call and try to alter your particular arrangements (within reason) to suit everyone.

It is kind of difficult to make the best possible pattern for your parents and yourself. There are a lot of variables to consider.

Some parents are eager to have equal time with their kids, so the kids spend two weeks at one house, two weeks at the other, or shift back and forth on some other equality-based schedule. This works very well for some kids, usually those whose parents get along well and live fairly near each other.

Some parents who live many miles apart make arrangements for the kids to live with one parent during the school year and move in with the other parent for the summer and longer holidays. Kids often enjoy the opportunity to have a different set of summer friends and activities, as well as an extended visit with their parent. Sometimes, though, they don't like this disruption in their own social lives.

All in all, most kids feel that the inconveniences of moving back and forth are worth it when the arrangement is working smoothly and helping them maintain current and strong relationships with both of their parents. Without regularly scheduled visits or home exchanges, some kids find that they begin to lose out on having a decent relationship with their nonresident parent. Sometimes there is nothing you can do about that.

Ideally, you need to be included in the decisions about how you are going to be dividing up your time, but with sensitivity on the part of your folks, this whole thing can be easier. You need to feel good about switching homes in order to benefit from it.

Tell your parents what will make that easier for you. They may not be able to meet all of your requests or needs, but they won't know what those are if you don't tell them.

- No one can tell you exactly *how* to feel good about switching homes. You need to figure that out.

- Again, with time, things will start to feel more normal.

- Regularly scheduled visits and changes make things easier, allowing you to plan your own life around a dependable schedule.

I switched houses every two weeks. I've got a brother who's two years older than me, and we did the whole thing together. He's the one person I've spent the most time with in my life and that was some sort of like a stable part of my life. I don't know how I made it more simple, I just sort of did it. There were complications, you know, like you leave things at one house and you've got to go back and you have to figure out how you're going to get there or whatever. It got a lot easier as soon as my brother started driving, because then we didn't have to depend on my parents driving. They lived about three miles apart, not very far, but far enough to make it a little difficult.

TRICIA, Age 17

My dad's more easygoing about things I do. Like he'll say, "Bring people over, stay out, don't tell me, it doesn't really matter, just do what you want to do." And my mom's like, "Tell me where you're going," plan, plan, plan. "You can only have this many people over and this many in your room...." Now it's hard, too, because we have to go and see each set of grandparents and each set of parents, and spend a good amount of time at each house. You have to divide all your time between all of your friends and your mom and your dad and your grand- parents. When they first divorced I spent Friday nights at my dad's. When he finally got a house we stayed there every other weekend, and Wednesday night for dinner. But it was flexible. They would switch weeks or whatever. And they talked about it with us and said, Is this cool? Sometimes it was a real pain in the neck to go back and forth. After we had spent a weekend at my dad's it was hard to go back to my mom's because my brother acted very different, real angry and testy. He just flipped out. I wasn't quite that bad, but it was hard to come back to my mom's. Wednesday nights were weird, because I'd get there and feel kind of aaaaaaaaah, and by the time I'd get to feeling normal it was time to go.

DONNA, Age 20

24

Give Your Parents' New Partners a Chance

You cannot make yourself feel something you do not feel, but you can make yourself do right in spite of your feelings.

—PEARL BUCK

If your parents are human, and chances are that they are indeed human despite what you may be thinking about them lately, they will in all probability date. Dating was discussed in Chapter 12, and it is a strange phenomenon. You should not, under normal family circumstances, be privy to your parents' love lives. This is disconcerting. What is likely to be even more disconcerting is when Mom and/or Dad decide they want to try the lifetime commitment thing again—with new partners. They want to start married life afresh and anew. You will probably feel pretty odd about that. They were married, then they weren't, now they are again? You want to tell them to make up their minds, to figure out their priorities. They clearly have no concept of this eternal bond of love thing, right? All of this may be true, but you are going to have to deal with it as well as you can.

Just because you have a new stepparent does not mean that this person has to take over the parenting role of a mom or dad. Nobody has really defined the "correct" role for a stepparent, though, so they usually kind of flounder around at the beginning. It would be wise and mature of you to give them a hand. It will make life easier for all of you if you can find a way to get along with your parent's new spouse. This may take some serious negotiating.

Naturally, your parent would like for things to go as smoothly as possible, but few new stepparents glide effortlessly aboard the family vessel without making some waves.

Some people get along really well with their stepparents, and others have found a way to ignore them almost completely. You should do whatever works in your situation. Yeah, this is a wimp-out answer to one of life's more complex and annoying questions, but the fact of the matter is that society has given us no protocol for dealing with our parents' serial spouses. If you're older and pretty much out of the house already it may be easy to establish a polite, distant relationship, if that's all you want. But when you are still growing up and you have to live in the same house as this totally random person who is now the next closest person to your parent, things can get tense. You might feel if you are too nice, you'll be betraying your other parent (not true: These should not be competitive relationships). If you are too cruel, you'll just be making life difficult for everyone. If you are somewhere in between, maybe you have not registered an opinion on the subject and are still having a hard time figuring out what you think. It is the easiest thing in the world to know what you are thinking, though. The hard part is trying to make that work with the rest of your life.

- It is easier to be nice than it is to fight constantly. In most cases it's easier to have little contact than negative contact.

- This new person is the person whom your parent has decided to try to spend the rest of his or her life with. Give the new person a chance, in the name of love, or whatever.

- You are under no obligation to like someone you don't like. You can, however, still get along with him or her enough to help keep the peace.

Having stepparents is good sometimes, but it can also be very bad sometimes. If there's any one thing that stands out as being the hardest thing about being a part of a divorced family, I guess that's it. They're just there. They arrive in your life and they tell you what to do. Sometimes it's a good thing. Sometimes it's a bad thing because they're overstepping their bounds or they say the wrong thing or do the wrong thing. By now I can work that out better. I think that the way it works with my stepparents is that as I get older I've gained their respect. They've started understanding that I can handle something by myself, whereas before they didn't really know me and yet they were trying to be parents to me.

JOHN, Age 19

My stepfather really didn't like me when he first met me. I was probably pretty spoiled at that time because everybody feels sorry for kids of divorce, so I imagine I was pretty spoiled. He was very strict and the most strict out of all of my parents. He became the discipline figure in my life. It went okay, you know, until you get older and you're a teenager and you start thinking things like, "You're not my father" and stuff like that. But it mostly was all right. He and my mom separated when I was 17 and that was harder for me than my parents because, you know, he'd lived in my house since I was a little kid. I'm still real close to him and care a lot for him. So he became like the third parent, and a real parent.

JILL, Age 28

25

It's Normal to Wish Your Parents Would Get Back Together, But They Probably Won't

I love my past. I love my present. I'm not ashamed of what I've had, and I'm not sad because I have it no longer.

—COLETTE

Change makes most people uncomfortable. We don't really like to have everything that is likable and familiar uprooted and moved around, especially our families. Instability just isn't one of the things that we seek out and reach for in our lives, yet here it is.

Feeling safe and secure within your family is one of those regular things that we tend to take for granted until it goes away. When your whole family is going through strange changes, you will probably wish that things would just return to "normal," go back to the way they were. A lot of people were not even aware there was any problem in their parents'

109

marriage until their parents made an announcement, dropped a bomb on the household, and started regrouping.

No one takes divorce lightly. This includes people with four or five of them under their belts. They all meant to make it, and it was a painful realization for them to decide that this marriage wasn't going to work. Usually, once they've announced their decision to divorce or once they've separated, it is far past the point of no return in their relationship and there is nothing anyone can do to bring things back to the way they were. In fact, the way things were before the divorce, if you think about it, is what made them get divorced in the first place.

You've just got to go with the flow, adapt to the changes in your situation, and accept that the divorce was going to happen no matter what. Think of it as an earthquake. There is nothing anyone can do about an earthquake, and there is no going back to the way things were before it happened. An earthquake may not be such a hot metaphor. Divorce is not by nature as destructive as an earthquake—it just shifts things around rather than shakes them to the ground. Keep in mind that after an earthquake, things sometimes are built back up stronger and better than they were before, but this metaphor has been taken too far already.

Yes (sigh), you are likely to hope that they'll get back together. You are not the only person who has had this thought. They probably won't do it, though, and it has nothing to do with you. They just can't be married anymore. Too much water under the bridge, dust in the wind, rainfall in everyone's life, and all that. It is time now to deal with them not getting it all back under one roof. Accept it and move on, for your health's sake. Deal with their being apart and with your life moving around for the moment like the red blobs in a lava lamp.

- It is totally natural to wish that things would get back to the way they were before.

- By the way, it is also natural and okay not to wish this.

- If they don't get back together, don't say nobody warned you. Try to make the best of your new situation.

I came in and my parents had gone out and gotten fried chicken. They sat me down and said that my dad was going to leave for a while and they didn't know when he was coming home, but he just needed to leave for a while because they were having some problems. I got really upset and he got really upset. It's the only time I've ever seen my dad cry in my entire life. It was really an emotional time. And then when it was all over, I'll never forget, all the food was cold and no one wanted to eat it. And I couldn't eat fried chicken for a long time after that. Then my parents hugged and my dad left. Back then the idea was that he was just leaving for a while, and maybe they thought they were going to get back together. He just took some clothes and a few possessions. I didn't know it then, but there had been problems for about three years. But it was pretty sudden for me. They didn't get divorced until last summer. They were separated for like ten years. My parents were so amazing through the whole thing. They were constantly there for me to talk about stuff with them. They didn't really fight or anything. After a while, when it became evident that they really were going to split up and my dad wasn't coming home, there were some hard times, but that didn't happen for a few years. So for the first couple of years when I was really adjusting to it things were really pretty easy. They were both really there for me.

NICK, AGE 20

My mom says the reason my dad and her got divorced was the alcohol, but with my stepdad, they were just a hassle to each other, plain and simple.... When my mother and stepfather divorced, I knew it was coming because holidays are a good time for my mom and divorces. I remember they had a big argument during my ninth grade year. It was the day before Christmas Eve. And she was saying, "I want a divorce." And I was like, "How can you do this? This is bullshit. It's Christmas." It was before the big Christmas party they always had every year. His boss would come over, a couple of other bosses, other people. So they said they had made up and went through that. They went back into therapy, and they went into some therapy with us. That was when I was 15 and I was starting to get high in that time period. They were constantly arguing. Half of my freshman year in high school. They got divorced at the beginning of my junior year. I remember because it was my birthday. That was when I turned 17. He came down and said, "If there's ever anything you want to talk about, you get in touch with me. Your mom's asked me to leave." I was like, "Okay. 'Bye." Shortly after that I was gone myself. At the time I wished they had stayed together, but they were going to do what they were going to do. It took me a long time to get straight with what I was going to do for myself. I'm in school now, straight for three years, pretty happy.

TIM, Age 22

When Matt, 19, was 11, his parents sat down with him and his older brother, who was then 13, to explain that they were going to separate.

"It was a little bit confusing," Matt says. "How could this happen to what I thought was a good couple where everything was fine? It just made me wonder what could have happened, whose fault was it, did I have anything to do with it, what were they thinking. Eventually I came up with answers to those questions, because they handled it very well. They always reassured me that it wasn't my fault or my brother's fault. They never fought in front of us. They never made it tough on us in any way, and eventually we understood that hey, their lives were better for it, they're happier. And their relationship with us didn't change, so why stay in a muddle about it?

"At first I wished my parents would get back together. First they said separation, but I realized really quickly that it was going to be permanent. I don't know how I realized it, I just came to terms with it and sort of stopped hoping for something that I knew shouldn't happen and couldn't.

"I think anyone would have some sort of worries, because it's a whole new thing. I mean your parents split up and what is going to happen? You don't know. I was worried. The first thing my brother asked was could he keep his room. I had no idea what was going to happen. I worried about whether things would be normal again, whether they were split up or together. I wanted to just sort of get back to some sort of comfort stage where you could just be comfortable with either of them and not have to deal with the problems of the breakup. I remember when they told me I had no idea, like wow, what's going on. But after a while things just sort of resolved themselves and I saw that my concerns were unwarranted—I realized that I hadn't done anything, that they could live apart, and I could still see them. Eventually I saw that neither of them was lost to me. It's just sort of moving around the parts instead of breaking them down.

"I could ask my parents questions. They were pretty open about it. But I guess I was more to myself about it. I could work a lot of things out by myself. I could see what was taking place for myself. I didn't confide in anyone. Only my brother. We sort of helped each other out. I didn't have to talk to my parents too much, because I could talk to him. So we kind of leaned on each other. He didn't know much more than I, but it sort of seemed like he did, and it was helpful.

"There were times when you just didn't want to be in the house. It was very tense in the beginning and you just sort of wanted to get away from it. You didn't want to have it all around you all day every day. You just sort of wanted to walk away and let it be over. Whether it was just going to a friend's house or going out with my brother, it was good just to get out and stay clear of things for a while.

"I didn't feel odd among my friends. They never made me feel like something was wrong, they just said, 'Oh, I'm sorry.' And it was fairly common, so there were a few who said, 'Yeah, me, too.' In some ways you sort of have to feel more drawn to other people who are going through this. It's just sort of something to relate with. You can be, oh yeah, you, too? Well, here's what happened to me. On a basic level you can just talk about it with someone who understands, whether it was another ten-year-old or eleven-year-old or someone older. It didn't necessarily give me answers when I talked to them, it was just comfortable, just something to talk about that we'd both been through. It's just like talking to someone who's from the same hometown or something. Now, it's so far past, now that my mom's remarried, now it's so much after the fact I don't feel I have to or want to look back on it, because everything's sort of worked out. I just tell people that my folks are divorced and my mom has remarried. It doesn't faze me. It does feel strange to say I'm going to my mom's wedding!

"The structure of our family is different now. Now it's about sharing time. Because I'm living with my dad I feel like I have to make an effort to go over to my mom's, to be with my mom sometimes because, you know, my dad, right now he's single and he can come see my brother's games or my games at school and it's easier for him and us to get together when we still live with him. So I guess it's just more of an effort to see my mom. I see my dad all the time when I'm home from school, living with him.

"The most my brother and I were ever caught in the middle was very minimal. My mom forgets to tell our dad something and expects us to tell him or him just to know, so there was some confusion with her having to get used to telling our dad, checking in with him before making plans. They weren't used to it. There were some times when we had to say, 'Hey, wait a second, I'm not supposed to work this out between you. Tell me what you want to tell me, I'm not going to mediate between you two.' But we never got caught in the middle. You just had to be aware of either side.

"My good memories—vacations, the holidays. I remember a trip to Europe when my whole family went and we have pictures. That was just a great time. We went to Hawaii once. Those times you just remember fondly, you remember it as a time when we were together and we were happy with it and we had a great time, and you don't really think about now, it's completely separate from it. You don't think, oh why couldn't it still be or, you know, none of that, just yeah, that was a great time and I was really happy with it. Nothing is messed up, the memory is still there. It's still real, just like other things in the past that won't happen again. We can still enjoy it even though it's passing, as most things are.

"When Mom's husband entered the picture: It was actually okay, and that's a lot because of his personality. He's a great guy, really easygoing. He was in an awkward situation coming into that. He was never pushy. He would try to be nice to us and make sure that we felt comfortable, but he would never try too hard. He was really good about it. Once he came along I was already over the initial shock and the pain, so . . . If it had been pretty soon after, it would have been really screwy, but he sort of gave enough notice. When they got married I'd already established a pretty solid relationship with him. When they got married he actually asked my brother and me first if it was okay, which, you know, was points with us. They're happy and that's what counts.

"I really had a sort of idealistic view of my parents, that their marriage was going to last. So their divorce made me aware that unexpected things can happen. In some ways it made me grow up faster. At eleven you're so raw, that's sort of a delicate stage. I guess if it happened to me now, I wouldn't have changed so much. It made me realize a lot of things, think about a lot of things, because you're sort of observing this 'adult' situation, this institution gone wrong, and you just sort of take it all in. You see that bad part of it, and you think what's the flip side of marriage, and what makes it go wrong? Most eleven-year-olds wouldn't be thinking about that.

"Of course, I don't want to get divorced. In one sense I want to do it better. I think, yeah, you know, I hope that doesn't happen to me. But also it's like what if that does happen to me? Either way I think this has made me realize it could help me. I could see maybe some of what was wrong and what they didn't do, so that it couldn't happen to me. And if it does happen, I can look at how they've handled it so well, so I guess I can handle it."

26

You're Going to Be Angry: Find Reasonable Outlets for Your Anger

When angry, count four; when very angry, swear.
—MARK TWAIN

Chaos, mayhem, your parents storming around the house changing your life with wild abandon, telling you things you probably don't want to hear, not telling you things that you ought to know. Of course you're going to get kind of irritable. You may feel overlooked, you may feel smothered, trod upon, toyed with, bounced around ... fill in the image of choice. Anger with being out of control of your own life, anger at being confused, trapped; that sort of thing can really get you down.

Repressing anger and holding it in can be so much more damaging than letting it out that it seldom seems worthwhile to hang on to it. Some people find that some kind of counseling helps them to deal with what is going on in their lives. They find it useful to talk to someone impartial who is on their side for the duration and can listen without telling anyone what they've heard.

Counseling is a healing resource for many people, but if you don't want to see a counselor or can't see one for some reason right now, you can find other ways to cope with your angry feelings. Ideally, you could just tell your folks what is bothering you and they could help you work it out. That may be part of the solution, even if they can't solve everything. Keeping your feelings from them probably won't help anything, but it may be easier to discuss how angry you sometimes feel at a time when you are calm and able to express your thoughts more clearly than you would be able to in the midst of a rage.

You can beat pillows, write poems, write nasty letters (think twice before sending them, though), make a lot of noise, dance really fast to loud music . . . the list goes on. It is imperative, though, to be careful not to take your anger out on those who don't deserve it, beginning with *you*. Do not inflict injury on yourself or put yourself in danger just to ease the pressure, or just to make people pay attention to how rotten you feel. You will only damage yourself and destroy your credibility as a reasonable person while you are at it. And try not to take out too much of your anger on your friends, either, if you want them to stick around.

Hopefully, you can be constructive in your expression. Destruction is no fun when you have to clean it up in the end, and even when it is someone else who has made you angry, you and you alone are responsible for your behavior. Don't do anything you may regret.

- Everyone is angry some of the time about lots of things, not just divorce.

- There are lots of different ways to deal with anger. Think constructively, not destructively.

- Don't ignore your angry feelings or try to keep them under wraps. That's a dangerous choice, like putting plastic wrap on a volcano.

Seeing the counselor was the main thing that got me past all my hostility and anger. It brought things to the surface and everything poured out. In some ways my mother had not really been there for me all through my childhood. And she admitted that, finally. I wanted her to be more of a mother, but she just couldn't do that. Counseling was a real lifesaver for me. I didn't go until I felt so depressed that I was willing to try anything. I only went three or four times, but it was enough to get me thinking along lines that I couldn't have come up with by myself. So I'm really glad that I had that opportunity.

KIMBERLY, Age 21

I would get really mad a lot, but I couldn't let that show with my dad. I used to take out all my anger and frustration on my mom because it was easy for me to do. We used to get into arguments a lot. But we're always cool about it. It's weird. Like she would start about something stupid like my socks or something stupid like that and we'd get into a big argument, and then, boom, it would be over and that would be it. We would get totally into cussing, then we would forget about it. Like we could really just blow off steam that way. My dad, though, would get offended. He had to maintain the authority figure, feel like he was in control. He'll always have to try and do it his way. When we'd get in arguments it would be just full on, like I'd end up saying, "I'm going to hit you." And it wouldn't be okay at the end. It wouldn't just blow over.

CHARLIE, Age 21

27

Being Spoiled by Parents or Relatives Won't Make Up for How Bad You Feel

You're depressed? Of course you're depressed. That's how you know you're awake.

—FRAN LEBOWITZ

A bunch of kids were sitting around a college dorm and talking about the toys that they had played with when they were younger. They ended up talking about the ones that they had always wanted but had been refused. One guy, Art, chimed in with, "Everyone always had that one friend with the divorced parents who had the big, expensive, loud toys. The only problem was that you could never find him because you never knew where he was staying."

It's kind of true. Most parents who get divorced feel pretty guilty about it and try to make it up to their kids. Not everyone tries to fix and make better by buying big, expensive gifts, but some do. Not infrequently it's the nonresident parent who tries to buy the affection of the kids. Parents are often confused about how to show they care. They are trying to show you they love you by getting you the things you want and by responding to your whims and material desires. They think that's the way to your heart. They are often mistaken.

Most kids quickly lose respect for people who try to trade gifts for affection. Giving and receiving gifts is a big pleasure in life. Even guilt-induced presents are fun. But gift giving alone can't heal a hurt or take the place of real communication between people.

You need to understand that those too big, too lavish guilt presents are not to be taken advantage of. Well, who wouldn't take advantage sometimes, let's face it. Just about everyone will take whatever is extended to them, especially when they are already shaken up and insecure about the position their family is in. But don't let it get out of hand. It will not make you feel better about your situation.

Some kids feel embittered and cynical about their family relationships because Dad gave them everything they wanted after he moved out. In these situations, Dad usually forgets to actually *say* that he cares. He thinks his message, however backhanded and hidden, is easily derived from his actions. But in this case, actions *don't* speak louder than words. You need to let him know that it is not enough to get stuff. You need care and real contact as well.

Similarly, the notion of "quality time" is pretty warped. The theory seems to be that since divorced kids spend less time with one parent, the time when they *are* together is more valuable. Parents sometimes try the strangest things to get a meaningful experience out of their time with their kids. They are trying, again, to show that they care, but it can come off as forced. It's not so easy to plan meaningful experiences. Your growing up experiences and the time that you spend with your family can't be divided up so easily into "quality time" and "normal time" (for lack of a better term). Do what makes you comfortable, and let your parents know if they are putting you in situations that make you feel bad.

Stepparents may try to smooth their way into their new family by being extremely generous to the kids. This is also known as bribery. You are under no obligation to like anyone who gives you things. You may feel obligated to be civil and polite when the gifts are given, but you should in no way feel pressed to like anyone for the stuff they give or don't give you. And if a gift makes you feel queasy, don't accept it. You'll never be able to enjoy it, so it's better to say, "Thank you, but I can't accept this."

- Some parents start to really spoil their kids when they get divorced. Recognize that this is usually caused by guilt—and tell them how you see it.

- Do not feel obligated to get along with someone because they have given you presents.

- You need to be shown that people, like your parents, care for you in *real* ways. Don't be afraid to tell them this.

I really didn't care for my stepfather. But you know, I had my mom and I had my dad on either side of town. I was a little kid, you know, third or fourth grade. It wasn't hard to impress me. Just give me ice cream and take me to play some basketball. It's not hard to impress a little kid—here, have a dollar, and wow! It didn't matter, though. It wasn't because of material things that I didn't like my stepfather. I pretty much got whatever I wanted and that's why when my parents were living in the same town it was so nice. If Mom wouldn't give it to me, Dad would. Sure, I took advantage of it.

Rob, Age 20

My father called today and he said, "So, I haven't talked to you all summer, when am I going to see you?" I said, "I have two days left. Everything that I have in the next two days is pretty firmly scheduled in." I told him what I had to do, which was pretty hectic, but I said, "If you want to have lunch on Friday, that would be nice." And he was like, "Is there any-thing you want now, you know, 'cause I haven't talked to you, so is there anything you want?" And I was like, "Well, I was out near your apartment the other day shopping for a car stereo." And he said, "I can buy you a car stereo." And I said, "I don't want you to do that. I mean I want one, but I'll ask for it for my birthday if I decide I want to get it from you." I don't know. I just feel kind of weird about him saying, "I haven't talked to you for a long time, do you want this?" It's just stupid. There are things that I want and things that I've been wanting to do, and sometimes I'm not sure, do I take them, do I not take them? I don't know why he's offering them and I don't know if he's rationalizing it in the same way that I am. I don't know if he thinks that's the way you do things. I think he might very well genuinely think that's the way people are. I just think there's something screwed up in his head big time.

Rebecca, Age 20

28

You Are Going to Grow Up Faster: In Some Ways It's a Real Advantage

The future is something which everyone reaches at the rate of 60 minutes an hour, whatever he does, whoever he is.

—C.S. Lewis

Witnessing the complete restructuring of your family is bound to alter the way you think about people. Sure, confusion, anger, and disillusionment are going to play key roles for a long while, but usually people come out of this whole mess with their heads on straight and some pretty good insights into the nature of people and their relationships with each other. Think about it: You have a front row seat for the critical scenes in what was supposed to be an eternal relationship. You are witnessing the reorganization of your immediate family. You will have a chance to learn quite a bit about your

126

parents, the rest of your relatives, yourself, and a little bit about the legal system.

Most kids whose parents have split up are pretty opinionated and vocal about what they think went on. They are likely to know more about what happened than their parents think. They have had to come to grips with a lot of stuff that most people their age don't have to think about. Some of these kids know a good deal about infidelity, most of them know how to cook, many of them know how to more or less take care of themselves and younger siblings, and everyone has had an opportunity to develop better interpersonal skills, which can't help but come in handy someday. Figuring out how to deal with your parents in their new roles, knowing who to ask for money and when, knowing who pays the medical bills and who is responsible for getting you to the dentist . . . the list of new coping skills can go on forever.

There is no such thing as a low-impact divorce. No matter how well it is handled by the parents, there are sure to be big issues to work out and changes that will affect your daily life. Whole worlds of new responsibility are suddenly tossed your way, along with big changes in what you can expect from the adults in your life. It is inevitable that you will grow up a great deal.

Don't knock it. The ability to take care of yourself, to have a mature understanding of the way things work in the day-to-day world, and to get things done in the midst of adversity are definitely advantages. You may not like everything that's happening, but you can get something useful out of it. The way you handle things now can help you come up with creative solutions to other problems for the rest of your life.

- Things are going to be rough, but surviving them will make you a stronger person.

- You are going to know more about people and how they work or don't work. This knowledge will always be useful.

- You will grow with change. Change and chaos are two of the major forces in the universe. It is a sign of maturity when you can handle them, at least most of the time.

My mother was sick a lot. She was in bed a lot of the time. And my father worked. Basically we never spent that much time together, but we did have dinner together every night. Then when I was ten my father moved into another bedroom. I remember I was worried that they were going to get divorced. I asked them if they were going to get a divorce and they said no. Nothing really changed. They were speaking to each other. But then as the years passed it got pretty . . . a sort of silent rage. The air was filled with anger and everybody absorbed it. We lived with another family. We moved in with them when I was 12. And my family had the upstairs and they had the downstairs. They didn't have the happiest family either. Eventually my father moved out and my mother and my sister and I moved down the street. It was better because we didn't have to deal with being around them. I hated my parents and I basically cut off any desire to be around them. I didn't know them as people at all. I went away for a year when I was 14 to live with some relatives. When I got back I saw my immediate family in a much, much clearer light than I had before, because I'd gotten some distance from it. I saw how my father was treating my mother and what my mother was doing, what my sister was doing. Suddenly like everything in the dynamic was just totally clear to me. And about myself, too. I was aware that I was looking down on my mother because she was quieter than my dad and was treating her badly in the same way my father was.

As soon as I realized that, the day, the second I realized that, I stopped. My mother, after the divorce and we were living in the apartment, I gained a lot of respect for her because she had been ill and in bed for most of our childhood and that last year before they got a divorce she was learning how to work with computers so she could get a good job. Here's this woman who suddenly has two kids, she's on her own with all this responsibility, and suddenly working. And I just gained immense respect for her. Not that we didn't have difficult times together, but ... Since I moved out four years ago I've just gone through phases of getting along with her. And my father, the same thing. It seems pretty clear, there were just two people that kind of grew apart. I did wish that, although it was nice of them to try to stay married—at least to stay in the same house—I guess they were waiting for us to get a little older. When it started getting really difficult I wish they had just divorced. Because even though divorce is really traumatic for younger children, I think it's more traumatic to have to live with really unhappy people.

LAURA, Age 22

My mother taught me about washing clothes and doing the dishes and keeping the house clean. You know, she wanted me to be one of those independent men, able to take care of myself. So you know when it was just me and her, I was used to it, you know I could cook a little bit. Hey, I could cook damn well! You learn to be very flexible. I was still pretty young, but I was growing up.

ROB, Age 20

29

You Have Nothing to Be Embarrassed About

No one can make you feel inferior without your consent.
—ELEANOR ROOSEVELT

Because divorce is so commonplace, you ought to damn well know that you are not remotely alone. No matter how strange and convoluted your family relationships and situations are at any given moment, rest assured that there are many others who are feeling the same way. Unless your situation is especially deranged, you are guaranteed that there are folks out there who are more confused than you are. Even if your situation *is* especially deranged, fear not.

Sometimes people feel embarrassed about not knowing exactly how things are going to work out. You may feel kind of silly for not knowing exactly what is going on in your own immediate family, or you may just feel kind of ashamed about your family splitting up. Hey, if all those other people can make it work out, you all must be strange or something, right?

130

Wrong. Every family is strange in their own special and unique way. At least your folks are aware and considerate enough to try to do something about it.

Divorce should no longer be considered an exercise in dysfunction. Divorce is more of an attempt to change the family structure to more fully and adequately fulfill the needs of all the family members. Face it: If your parents haven't been happy to be together, you have not been living in a happy household. What's the great advantage of preserving *that?*

What's wrong with the pursuit of happiness? Why should you feel bad because your parents are trying to improve the chances for the happiness of everyone in the family? How is this embarrassing?

If you are alone in your group of friends, or even in a real minority by having divorced or separated parents, you should count yourself lucky. You have a rare insight into many facets of human nature that these other kids won't get a good look at until they are much older. You have probably been thinking about some really heavy issues and therefore have a good head start on that kind of thing. Anyone who tries to make you feel silly or ashamed about the state of your family is horning in on something that is none of their business. Actually, you should feel free to hold forth on the personal growth that you have accomplished due to your circumstances even if you don't believe a word of it yourself.

So your parents couldn't make it work. Big deal. At least they are not kidding themselves into thinking that an empty marriage is better than no marriage at all. You ought to think of yourself as lucky that they knew enough to call it quits.

None of this is to say that you ought to think of your family as superior to those that have managed to stay under one roof. Why does everything have to be good, better, or best? It is just how things worked out for you all. Just as there are many different variations on the theme of divorce, there are many different types of families that have stayed together, each with their redeeming features. Most kids don't talk about how their parents are still married and how much that has taught them about love and devotion. At least they don't talk about it in casual conversation. So you shouldn't feel you have to explain or defend your family either—unless there's some particular reason why you want to. If you find yourself justifying your family constantly, getting defensive about how you live, and doing both with little to no provocation, you are displaying a serious lack of self-confidence about your family's way of life. Showing that you are not embarrassed does not mean you have to get vocal and militant. Chances are that few people care all that much about the intricate workings of the divorced family.

- Why get embarrassed? Every family is strange. At least yours is open about it.

- There is nothing bizarre about having divorced parents. Check it out, there are fewer "normal" families than you may think.

- Be suspicious of anyone who tries to make you feel bad about your parents' divorce. Why should they want to hurt you?

I was the only person from my parents' marriage, so I felt really protective of that, and I felt, you know I never had this big conflict about wishing my parents were married or anything, but I always just kind of felt protective of my name. I was the only one in my house with my [last] name. I always wanted people to know that I wasn't one of them. I was glad to be different, unique. I never felt like it was a weird thing that my parents were divorced. I guess it never felt like I was the only one. I don't know if I was or wasn't. But I just always felt like I had lots of Christmases and lots of birthdays.

JILL, Age 28

I was so ashamed. I didn't want anybody to know. No one in high school knew what I was going through. I'd enter a contest in art. I would win. I would show up, get my prize, I would go home, and no one knew that I was basically going nuts.

TARA, Age 23

It's kind of strange for me to be in a house where people are still married and everything seems so happy. Actually, I have a few friends where their families really are normal. You think that there's no such thing as a functional family, but I think that there is and it's so strange to be at dinner with them, because they all sit around and make jokes and they laugh at them and they do normal things. And I'm like, oh my God, it's so strange, I haven't done this for years. But I've never felt out of place, because I know that divorce is such a common thing now.

TRICIA, Age 17

30

If You Have Brothers and Sisters, Form Alliances with Them

There can be no situation in life in which the conversation of my dear sister will not administer some comfort to me.

—LADY MARY WORTLEY MONTAGU

When the whole structure of your life is changing all over the place, it is good not to have to go it alone. If you have brothers and sisters you may find it extremely helpful to talk to them about what is going on. Since no two divorces are alike, having someone who is caught up in the same divorce as you are can help serve as a reality check, as well as good moral support. And, since no two people are alike, your siblings may have different and helpful insights into the experiences you are sharing.

When two or more of you have the same problems and difficulties and can voice the same concerns to your parents or others who can help you, you may arrive at solutions more easily and quickly. It is easier to work with your family rather than to try to do without your family. This is not to say that you should try to turn your brother or sister into your best friend when you don't get along. But since you are inevitably sharing this divorce and dealing with the same (probably crazy) family, you have pretty much the same problems and the same need for solutions.

Maybe your brother or sister has noticed something that you haven't. Maybe he or she can answer a question that you don't feel comfortable asking your parents. You can learn from each other and figure out what is going on when things get really strange. You can escape together if things are really bad and hang out together when they're okay and you just want some company.

Of course, you won't go through this big change like Siamese twins. Each of you will have some unique reactions to the divorce, and you won't be able to share everything. Your ages and your individual relationships to each of your parents will make for differences. And if you have brothers and sisters, you already know how easy it is for siblings to get on each other's nerves, especially when everything else is kind of stressful. Still, you should try to take advantage of the help that's available in bailing out the family ship whenever you feel swamped. After all, they're in the same boat.

- Try talking to your brothers and sisters if you feel like it and think it might help, even if you haven't talked very intimately before. They may have something interesting to say.

- You don't have to agree with everything they say. Everyone has a different take on any given situation.

- Know when to leave your siblings alone and when to

have them leave you alone. Don't build unhelpful
dependencies.

*I've talked to my older siblings a lot. They understand my mom
and dad just as well as I do. I think that having siblings is the
best thing in a divorce. I can't imagine doing it alone. We all
had our own ways of dealing with the divorce and it was really
separate. It wasn't the sort of thing that you go through together, supporting each other the whole way. We all had to
learn from the experience and just deal with it.*

TRICIA, Age 17

*My brother has a totally different relationship with my father
than I do. Like, he always went out of his way to hang out
with Rich. Rich hated it. He wished that my father would act
like he did toward me, also because he didn't like the fact that
he was being favored. My brother really resented how my father
treated me. My brother's pretty into fair and even stuff. We
talk about it a lot, Rich and I do, and until this past year we
haven't agreed a lot about stuff, but now he seems to agree
with a lot more things that I've been saying. I don't know if
I've changed or he's changed, but we've been agreeing more
about family and things.*

REBECCA, Age 20

31

Don't Let Anyone Speak Ill of Either of Your Parents

It is almost impossible to throw dirt on someone without getting a little on yourself.

—ABIGAIL VAN BUREN

There is a distinct possibility that your folks will be none too pleased with each other during and following their divorce proceedings. This is nothing unique. It is much more rare for people to find ways to be nice to each other after they are divorced than it is for them to wish each other far, far away. People who divorce are rarely prepared for the sacrifices they have to make in order to get out from under a failed marriage. The bitterness that ensues from feeling cheated in a relationship can make things sticky for everyone involved.

Unfortunately, you are involved, at least by default, in the things going on between your parents. Sorry, but it kind of works that way no matter how old, young, or in-between you are.

You may hear all kinds of horrible speculations made about your parents. Wildly inaccurate suppositions about their actual species are pretty common ("He's such a pig!" "What a snake she is!"). None of this is any fun, because you are still related to both of these people, human or not.

You are completely within your rights to tell *anyone*, from your grandparents on up or down, that you don't want to hear disparaging things about either of your folks. Anyone who doesn't respect your wishes, once you make them known loudly and clearly, has major problems of their own. If someone is making you feel bad, challenging your loyalty to either of your parents, or irritating you with things they say about any members of your family, you ought to feel comfortable telling them that you don't like hearing those kinds of things and that you would appreciate it if they would just keep their thoughts to themselves. It is possible to make your point without being rude; to start by asking rather than demanding is a well-advised tactic. If, however, after you have politely requested that someone stop saying such things, he or she still persists in being an inconsiderate beast, you may then feel free to throw one of those tantrums that make people point at you and whisper, "Broken home." More power to you.

All kinds of people like to mind your business, especially when something like a divorce comes up and gives them a good excuse to zero in on you. Teachers have been known to butt in uninvited, so have family friends, new relatives, plumbers ... the list goes on and on. The truth is that none of them can know what is going on in your life as well as you do; if they are bashing someone you care about they are hardly being helpful. No matter what your own judgments are about your family, none of us likes to hear other people offer negative opinions of our close relatives. This is just a human nature thing. People tend to be loyal to those whom they've grown up caring about.

There's also a way in which this has nothing to do with your family's divorce. It just isn't courteous to say nasty things about someone's family members. You are entitled to common courtesy—just like everyone else. Welcome to civilization. Your family relationships are not public domain just because your family has been reorganized. So tell those people to stop!

- Some things just aren't the business of other people. They should be politely reminded to mind their manners.

- Don't worry about whether you are being hypersensitive. If something bothers you, you are perfectly right to try calmly to do something about it.

- There is nothing wrong with defending *your* feelings, even if you don't feel especially loyal to your parents.

I don't want to feel like I favor either of my parents, and I don't. I try to keep that sort of on a joking level. I've put my limits up. There was one time when my father was going to drive me home and he had drunk something and I didn't want to get in the car with him because he was drunk and I said, "I'll take a cab home." He got really defensive. His wife turned to me and said, "Tricia, just because your mother's an alcoholic doesn't give you the right to yell at your father for having a glass of wine." And I just said, "I don't want to hear that. I don't want to hear you interpret my mother's alcoholism. I'm not doing this because my mom's an alcoholic. I'm doing this because I don't want you to drive me home."

TRICIA, Age 17

When people told me bad things about my father, I felt really ashamed. Because my father had been really looked up to. He was in law enforcement. He was protective service to superstars. I could say to my friends, "Hey, we had a call from Eddie Van Halen to ask us to come out and visit him." I was part of these things. Then when my dad started doing this stuff and getting into the paper with one thing and another, I felt really screwed up. . . . My last name is the same as his and I was associated with it, so are people going to think badly of me now? That was my big worry, the repercussions of Dad and his actions on me. My mom helped me by saying that I was very special. Everything she said to me, if I didn't hear it then, I heard it later. You don't see those things, but when you look back on them, you suddenly understand. My mom just took it. She was so patient. This is when you learn what unconditional love is.

TARA, Age 23

You Are Not Responsible for Your Parents: They Are Adults

*Every human being on this earth is born with a tragedy
... that he has to grow up.... A lot of people don't have
the courage to do it.*

—Helen Hayes

It may seem unlikely at times, but your parents should be able to take care of themselves. With the drastic shifting around of the family and with all of the emotional stuff that you are all going through, chances are that your parents will try to depend on you for more than you can handle.

Lots of times kids start feeling responsible for their parents and start taking better care of them than they do of themselves. You all need to be there for each other. But your life is changing just as drastically as theirs, and you should not put yourself in a position to be leaned on too hard when you yourself are fragile.

Your parents may be moody, they may be crabby, they may

141

just be angry, but none of this is your fault and therefore none of it is your responsibility. Sure, you could consider yourself obligated not to bring on any more emotional trouble, but that's all you really have to do.

Parents usually come in a set so they can take care of each other without inflicting extra stuff on their kids. With the splitting of that pair there is bound to be some emotional outpouring. Chances are that you don't really want to hear about how the divorce is wrecking your mother's self-esteem. Regardless, you are probably going to hear a bit more about it than you want to. You should feel free to support your parents and listen to them as far as you feel comfortable. If you actually want to do this, wonderful, but it is not your job to keep your folks on their feet. There may come a point when you just can't handle it anymore. And you shouldn't have to. Stand firm. You are the child and they are the parents; it is not your responsibility to hold them together or to lead them through this tough time. If they're not doing so well, tell them you are worried about them and want them to find someone to talk to, preferably a professional counselor.

Guilt is also one of the things that we need to talk about here. Whatever they did during the marriage, however long they stayed together for the sake of the children, whatever it is that they have done that is now making life more difficult than it needed to be, is not your fault. It is the responsibility of the adult in any relationship to make sure that they are doing the best they can with what they've got. Poor judgment on the part of your parents is not your fault. Their loneliness is not for you to solve. Their anxieties and wishes for someone else to share the load are also not your problem. It is the duty of the parents to take responsibility for their own actions and to move on from there, doing the best that they know how. It is not your job to lead your parents. It is their job to take care of business.

- Do not feel guilty for the things that your parents have done.

- They will probably confide in you. This is fine as long as you don't mind. When you mind, say so.

- You should not feel responsible for the actions of your parents; it is their life, and you are the child. They should feel responsible for you.

Unfortunately there are some parents who don't take care of their children once they get a divorce. You know, Pop thought he was divorcing me, too. Unfortunately that's not true. He wasn't that bad at sending the money. All I had to do was just call up and ask. But, my mom . . . she's not the type to be like, "I'm gonna take you to jail." I didn't feel like I should have had to call him. I'm his son. He should just call and be like, "How's it going?" He shouldn't be making me take care of him. When I need money I call my dad, basically that's our relationship. Whenever I need money I call my dad, and my mom takes care of everything else. And then, as I got older, my mom really just took care of everything. That's why I love her.

ROB, Age 20

I felt really responsible for my mother. It was me she stuck with the relationship for. Why would anyone want to stay with a relationship like that? So I went through a guilt period where I couldn't even talk with my mom because I felt too bad. So we went from one extreme to another with me yelling at her, then not talking to her. I just didn't want to hurt her any more than she'd already been hurt.

TARA, Age 23

*I get along pretty good with my mom. I give her a lot of credit.
She's a single mother, she has her own business, she works
hard. She's the one basically putting me through college. I went
to a private high school, and tuition was pretty expensive. The
thing was for my dad to pay half, and my mom would always
have to end up paying his half, like begging him to pay her. I
think my dad was a little jealous of my mom having her own
business. He has his own business, too, but he always tells me,
"I work so hard, I work so hard and I never can get ahead."
His hands are just like calluses. He does work hard. He gets
up at five and comes home at eight and goes to bed at nine and
gets up the next morning. Every day. He just gets sick and
tired of it. I feel bad for him. Sometimes I get scared because I
think he's going to do something to himself. He always tells me
he wants to get away. He always tells me, "We're going to go
on vacation sometime. One year for Christmas we're going to
go away. We'll go skiing or something." That's one thing, when
we were younger we used to go skiing every Friday night with
some other friends. We used to go camping. Now I go camping.
My parents are too busy. You know, when I was younger my
dad would drag me along, and now I'm dragging my dad along,
saying, "Come on, Dad, let's go skiing or something."*

JEFF, Age 19

Allison remembers being in third grade when her parents divorced. Her younger brother was three years old, and her sister was two. "We started going to see my dad on weekends and every other Wednesday or whatever," Allison says. "For me, I was really attached to my dad. My little sister thought it was weird, because she was only two and had to go to this strange man's house. So I think it was harder on them.

"My grades dropped big time. They put me in resources and gave me all these tests and stuff and said, 'Well, she's bright, she's not stupid, why is she in here?' It was just weird.

"I had a stepdad who came onto the scene shortly after my dad was gone and luckily he was a really nice guy. He's still around and we all love him. He's never been my dad, but he's a good guy.

"Then my dad met a woman who had four kids. So all of a sudden we have all these brothers and sisters. We were all different ages, all had different fathers. Her kids had three different fathers. Her history was really bad. That was hard. They all kind of thought we were snotty little kids, because they had been molested and stuff. Two of them are older than me, about three and two years. Then there is a little boy who is probably three years younger than me, and a little girl who is four years younger than me.

"We would be together whenever we spent the weekend. They had all moved in together into a house. I kind of felt like I was intruding when I was there and not accepted at all. We lived in a nice house on a nice side of town and had our friends and went to school and had life pretty easy. It was just awkward. They didn't have much money, and they were all crowded. We didn't work things out for a long time. My dad and his wife are very strict people, and my mom's really laid-back and basically lets us do what we want to do. We have expectations, but not nearly as much as at my dad's.

"He ended up moving to Montana. We lived in Utah. He took his family to Montana, and at the time my mom and I weren't getting along very well, and I ended up moving to Montana with him. Just me, not my brother and sister. I was thirteen. I lived there for six months until I decided to move home. My dad and I really haven't talked for about the last four years. I probably haven't seen him in three and a half years. He was upset. We can't just have our dad, we have to have him and the rest of his family, and if we don't accept all of them and everything that they do and say, then forget it. He basically said, 'If you guys want any contact, you contact me.' My sister wrote him a letter and tried to explain how she felt, but she's only thirteen now. She wrote to him about a year ago or so. He wrote back kind of a nasty letter saying, 'You didn't include Tamara and the kids, blah blah blah.' And she said, 'Well, I don't want Tamara and the kids, I want you. You're my dad and I don't care about them.' But he will never accept that.

"We all fought a lot and disagreed on things and didn't get along. The hardest part for me was when I was living in Montana with them. I have a lot to thank my stepmom for, she really helped me out a lot. But when it comes down to it, I really don't like her very much. I tried really hard, and she tried really hard. My dad would treat me differently than the other kids. If I got in trouble he'd take me off to the side and say, 'Don't do that.' If they got in trouble he'd tell them in front of everyone. He was more gentle with me. You know, I'm his little girl and I guess he was nicer to me.

"My older stepsisters both got pregnant at eighteen and moved out. They'd run away many times. They've got this awful history and sometimes I think, 'Do I really know these people?' And I know them very well. So I was kind of there for my youngest stepsister. I was kind of like the sister she never had. That was really weird for me. As much as I loved her, she just drove me crazy because she was so hyperactive, asking me questions all the time. I'd get annoyed with her. I tried really hard not to blow up, so it was a lot of, 'Be nice to Carly,' and 'You're not any better than they are.' And I never thought I was better than they are. My stepmom, and later my dad— My dad's changed a lot. He was almost brainwashed by this woman. When I finally left, he was saying, 'Oh yeah, you're going to go back to Utah, you're going to drop out of high school, you're going to be pregnant by the time you're eighteen.' And I'm thinking, Is that all you're thinking of me? He was thinking I was the same as them, and I wasn't. Here I am now in college, I graduated from high school, got scholarships, and I kind of want to say, 'Hey, look at me now. Maybe you'd be proud of me.'

"He basically disappeared from his whole family. I've always had contact with his family, my cousins and uncles and aunts. He completely quit writing everybody, cut it off completely. He's in his own little world in Montana somewhere. His own dad didn't know where he was. They'd call us and say, 'Where's your dad?' I'd say, 'I don't know. Did he move?' Come to find out, he did move. I called his wife's parents, who are really nice people. I said, 'I'd like to get in touch with my dad.' They gave me an address and number.

"When I was graduating from high school, I just sent him an announcement to say that I was graduating and he wrote back, basically giving us a major guilt trip—the three of us. Like, we haven't contacted him and we don't love him. Basically toward the end he was saying that I don't even have the capability to love, that I don't even know how. That really hurt.

"I kind of just go on with my life. I'm going to school. I'm happy with myself, so I don't worry about it as much. I wish he could understand my point of view. I wish he could listen. Because I could tell him and tell him until I'm blue in the face, but he's not going to hear it. I'd want to say that I'm not all those awful things that he expected me to be, or that his wife expected or told him I was. That I'm a good person. I'd like it if he'd acknowledge that. Just to acknowledge it and get off of this guilt trip. I'd like for him to grow up.

"I've got my family, my brother and my sister and my mom's side of the family. I've got my dad's family and my stepdad's family, too. They are really supportive and help me out with what I need and tell me I'm a good person and tell me I'm doing a good job. They're there for me. It's kind of like my father's just gone. And I've kind of like accepted the fact. The only problem I've had lately with that is that I'm coming to that age where marriage is actually an issue and I'm wondering, well, is my dad going to be at my wedding? Is that going to be weird if my dad's not there? He won't ever see my children grow up. I don't know. I feel bad for him missing out on it, and I feel bad for my kids missing out on it.

"My stepfather fills in a lot. He works an awful lot. To tell you the truth, after living with him for probably nine years, it's only the last two years that I've even gotten to know him at all. He was there, but we didn't sit down and have major heart-to-hearts or anything. In the last couple of years we'd go to school and to work together, you know, drive there, so we'd talk twenty minutes every day at least, and that was good time. I actually got to know this guy I've been living with for nine years. He's a really neat person. He's really together. He's really smart. He's something you can hold on to, which is nice. If you have a problem, he's there for you. You can go to him and he'll help you, and I guess he has replaced my dad, but he's still not a dad. I don't know how to explain it. For my little brother—I don't know. We've always had this weird thing with him where our stepfather is there being our dad, doing all the things a dad would do, supporting us, going to games, going to whatever, being in his place, but it's still—I don't know. I mean, we were so close to my dad for so long that I couldn't really picture my stepfather as my *dad*. I think it was really hard for my brother. My dad's a real outdoors kind of mountain guy, and he's also an artist. He wants to go shoot his bow and go hunting. And my little brother wants to play with the computer and ride horses. My stepdad is really into computers. It's weird, it's like my stepbrother should be with my dad and my brother should be with my stepfather. It's like it was meant to be. But my brother wanted to be accepted by my dad so badly and he just never was. And that was really hard on him. Probably in the past three years my brother's finally come into his own and is comfortable with himself. He's now fourteen.

"In third grade when the divorce was going on my mom had a real mental breakdown. She'll admit it now. She lived at the shrink's office. Basically it was my little brother and sister and I home with the baby-sitter. When the baby-sitter wasn't there, it was me. So I grew up really fast. Here I am eight years old and I have a three-year-old and a two-year-old as my kids almost, waking them up for school, making dinner, whatever. She wasn't there. So it's taken me a long time to get to the point where I can be a sister, not a mom. My mom would call me from work and say, 'Tell your brother and sister to do their homework.' And I'd say, 'No. You tell them to do their homework. I don't want to fight with them all the time.' Because that's what it would turn out to be. They'd say, 'You're not my mom.' I'm like, 'Hey, like I asked to be.' I don't want to be their mom, because they're a pain. She still plays the bit of, 'I'm a working mother. I don't have time for this. I love you very much, but please realize I'm a working mother' and all that. And I say, 'Yeah, you are, but you've got three kids.' And she's doing better with it."

Allison says her mother was really shocked when she moved to Montana.

"Here I am, her daughter, saying, 'You're not a good mom. I'm leaving. I don't care what you do with my brother and sister, I'm getting out.' She's really turned into the mom I've always wanted. So that turned out to be a really good thing. It was the lack of attention and caring that made me leave.

She'd almost buy us off. She wasn't there, so when she was she'd buy us stuff. And I didn't want the stuff, I wanted my mom.

"When I was there with my dad—I'd always put my dad on this pedestal. My dad's perfect. Well, my dad's not perfect and I learned that. I finally figured out my parents aren't perfect. I think little kids want to think that. Their parents can do no wrong. They're like gods. I found out he's a real human being and has problems. He kind of fell off his pedestal.

"My dad has this thing about how he didn't want to be the dad you go to on the weekend and he spoils you rotten and then you go back to your mom. So he made it kind of hellish. He took it too far. We'd go to his house and either be bored out of our minds or be working our butts off. He was like a slave master and it was kind of like child labor. It was bad. I can clean a house from top to bottom best you've ever seen it. He was ridiculous, like doing the dishes for three hours to get them perfect. He's a perfectionist. It's actually taken me a long time to try to get out of that—that it's okay if I throw my clothes on the floor. It's funny, because my room had always been absolutely perfect and when I came home from Montana, for like months you couldn't get from my door to my bed. It was just like total freedom. Now I think I've reached that happy medium.

"My mom used to tell us we should listen to our dad and respect him. And my dad was saying, 'Oh, she's a total bitch, blah blah blah. Don't listen to a word she says. She's a witch and her whole family is black widows.' One day I just told him, 'Don't talk bad about my mom. She's my mom and I love

her. If you've got problems, fine, but I don't want to deal
with it.'

"It was awkward. I kind of tried to step out of it and look
at the whole thing. I learned to put myself in other people's
shoes. I put myself in my stepsisters' position—what would it
really be like to have your dad totally walk out on you, be
pregnant when you're eighteen, run away. I put myself in my
dad's shoes and look at it and I can see where he would see
me as a spoiled brat. I can see that. And what can I do to
change it? I came to realize after a while that I'm just a normal
person, whatever is normal for me.

"I think a family should be a support group for each other.
I think that's what we all need, just somebody there for us,
people who care. I have many families, like my boyfriend's
parents are almost just as much my parents as my
parents are, and my ex-boyfriend's parents are kind of my
family, too. As far as I'm concerned, I've got kind of a large
family. It's just anybody who loves you. It's that love between
people that makes a family. I consider a lot of my friends
family. It's important that people have somebody to depend
on."

33

Look for the Up Side of Changes You May Not Want to Make in Your Life

Two men look out through the same bars:
One sees the mud, and one the stars.

—FREDERICK LANGBRIDGE

One of the things that everyone has to face during the division of households is the fact that life is going to change, like it or not. Some parents have the means, imaginations, and options of making these changes as easy and minimal as possible. One family we've encountered, wanting to keep their kids from feeling shuttled around, rented separate apartments for each parent. They took turns every other week moving back into the family home, where the kids remained. But even in that pretty luxurious situation, the kids experienced change and upheaval.

Redesigning home life means that the place where you have

probably always found the most security and sameness is suddenly insecure and not at all the same. All change brings on a period of strangeness, while new procedures, new rules, and mechanics are being worked out. Your home life will gradually take form and new routines will be established.

Every situation has good and bad features. Certainly your family's old routines weren't all hunky-dory. You adapted to how things worked then, and you will now adapt to how things work when your parents are no longer together. It's a big adjustment, but you will help yourself through it by looking for its advantages.

Some people find it useful to be able to move from one parent's home to the other's, whether it's on a weekly basis or every summer. Each household offers a break from the routines of the other—new scenery, new options for activity. Kids who have had to change schools may not be happy about leaving their friends, and who can blame them? But they'll help themselves feel better faster if they're willing to look into what advantages the new school might have. Maybe this school has a great track coach or a good theater department. Maybe it offers you a chance to make friends with people who don't remember what you looked like when you had braces or that stupid mushroom haircut.

It's a lot about attitude. You're being swept up in something you did not plan on and probably didn't want. The one thing you have at least *some* control over is your attitude. So when you can (and you won't always be able to), try to remember that there's an up side to every situation, a silver lining in every cloud, a redeeming feature to every arrangement, and as long as we're at it, there are more fish in the sea, more pebbles on the beach, every rose has its thorn, and the creamy filling always ends up on one side of the cookie no matter how you twist it.

- Changes in your life are what you make of them. You can make them work out for you or against you. Do the best you can with what you've got.

- Things are going to be strange at first, but they will settle down into a new kind of normal.

- Things are going to stay different from "the old days," but different doesn't have to be completely negative.

Right now I'm a very mobile person. I adjust to different situations very easily. You know, I was just in Spain for a year, and it wasn't a very difficult step for me. I mean, it obviously wasn't easy, but I was used to moving around and being in different situations. I'm used to change. So the divorce affected my life in that way. It makes me more of an open person, I think, probably just more able, independent. So that's one of those things I'm grateful for.

                                                    TRICIA, Age 17

My mom and I moved because my dad is in a wheelchair and the house is all set up for him. We had the house built and we had ramps put in and doors widened and all this stuff. It was easier for him to stay there. It was kind of assumed that I would be with my mom. . . . My parents get along better now than they did before. They still have to talk about things like bills and things for me. The first Christmas after they got divorced they both bought each other Christmas presents and I was like, "What are you guys doing? You're divorced. You're not supposed to do these things." My mother will say, "Why don't you go see your dad, you haven't been with him in a while." They're not best friends, but they're not—my dad doesn't resent me for living with my mom or anything. We don't do anything with all of us together anymore, but we never did before, except for those little family things where you're supposed to be like a happy family. We'd go in the car and they'd be bitching at each other and we'd get out of the car and they'd be smiling, hi, it's good to be here. Then we'd get in the car and they'd both be complaining again. . . . A lot of people I know say it was better when their family finally did this and stopped trying to pretend that they were getting along. I like the house I'm in now better because it's closer to all my friends and because I don't have to have a provisional driver's license here. So in some ways it's better living with my mom now. My best friends can just stop by now and they could never do that where we lived before.

BETSY, Age 18

34

Take Some Responsibility for Your Relationships with Your Stepparents and Stepsiblings

The human heart, at whatever age, opens only to the heart that opens in return.

—MARIA EDGEWORTH

Most parents date, and many remarry and all that other fun stuff. With the enormous number of divorces taking place in our culture in recent years, it is only natural that some of these families will end up combining into strange and gangling units.

All kinds of relationships are standard now that were uncommon not so long ago. There are stepparents, ex-stepparents, half sisters, stepsisters, ex-stepsisters.... It's all pretty strange and confusing. One of the reasons that families that have been through at least one divorce tend to get together with other similar families is that they have something in common. There

157

is shared ground, common bumbling, and confusion. Everyone involved has dealt with a major change in life that is unlike other changes. It's easier to understand each other when you have all been there.

For your parents, "recently single" is a nice thing to have in common when they first get out on the dating field. It always makes for a good story and something to chat about over dinner. That's why they all seem to find each other.

If your parents remarry you will certainly end up with stepparents and possibly with stepsiblings, too. This is going to be weird. If anyone tells you that there's nothing weird about it, they're wrong.

You used to have two parents. They were a unit. Then you had two parents who were no longer a single unit, but two units. Then you had two parents and their assorted spouses and the offspring of those spouses. This may be further complicated when one parent and a stepparent have a child who becomes your half sibling.

Some kids get to be very close with the kids of their stepparents. Others just know each other by name and don't really have much of a relationship at all. Neither of these situations is odd. Every family has different circumstances that make their different situations, well, different. You may be too old to start a real family kind of feeling with the kids of your stepfather. They may be too young, too hippie, too rich, too strange, too dorky, or too cool for you guys to get along as well as your folks would like. If they live with you some or part of the time, they are on your turf (or you are on theirs), but not at your invitation. It's complicated.

These kids are the close relations of a stranger who has appeared and become a reasonably permanent fixture in your house. Maybe you wonder just how permanent *this* one is going to be anyway, so you don't want to invest a lot of effort in getting to know the "steps."

You are allowed to not like any of the people whose title begins with "step," but this does not give you free reign to make life more difficult than necessary. You are under no obligation to be best friends, or even to feel and act like a sister or brother to your steps. You do have to be civil. They had as little say in this family thing as you did.

Stepparents are another story. They *mean* to be there, so they can be held accountable. Keep in mind though, that as you work things out with your stepparent, it is in your best interest to keep things as nonconfrontational as possible. Little ground is won in a big brouhaha with a stepparent. It just delays the truce, which is the only worthwhile goal if you want to get on with your life.

A lot of people find it difficult to get along with stepparents. They always seem to arrive before you are ready to deal with the situation. There is really no good time for them to show up. They are going to interfere with the closeness that you shared with your parent, and they are going to take up some of the time and attention that you probably need and want no matter how long your parents have been split.

You may not even like them as people. This does happen. Sometimes kids are accused of being jealous, of trying to be difficult, of not wanting their parents to be happy when the fact is that they just flat out don't like the new addition. Even if you don't like them, you're better off doing your part to get along well enough not to make things more difficult. What's the point of making the atmosphere at home hellish? Chances are that they want to get along with you, too. This may necessitate some negotiation between the two of you, to work out the terms that will allow the stepparent to give you as much independence and freedom as you need and to avoid arguments and conflict. This will call for tremendous maturity and self-control on your part. Good luck!

- You don't have to accept stepparents as parents, but they are a part of your home life now and you need to arrive at mutual respect.

- Your relationship with your stepsiblings will have to be shaped by you. You can be as close or as distant as feels right to you, no matter what anyone else wishes it would be.

- You are under no obligation to like anyone, just to get along well enough to avoid unnecessary conflict.

My stepsisters and brothers were never actually in our lives, so they'd come and visit once in a while and it was like, "Oh, hi, you're my brother by marriage." Nothing ever really clicked. There was just some tension there. We're related but not really. There's no connection. We were all very different, and I didn't even meet my stepsister until six or seven years after my stepfather and mother were married because she lived out in Oregon, I think, and all of his children had gone through college and were older and were getting married and there was just no common ground. I think I had a couple of conversations about music or something like that with his youngest son, but he was, I think, 28 when I first met him and I was just starting my teens. . . . I have a half sister, though, who is about 12 years younger than I am, and I am completely wild about her. I've been with her for her whole life and to me there is absolutely no difference between her and my older sister. They are both my sisters.

JOHN, Age 19

My dad has another daughter from his second marriage, and my brother is from my mom's second marriage. But that is one thing that I've always been happy about. I've never been sad about my situation except that my father and I have a bad relationship. Other than that I've never regretted my life being this way because I felt like if it didn't happen I wouldn't have my brother and sister growing up. They are my very favorite people and I really feel lucky. The thing that I like about having this kind of family is that you wouldn't know all these other people. Like my stepfather has two daughters from a previous marriage. I wouldn't know them, and they're great. And like their mother is really cool. My stepmother's family is really nice. You meet all these people. Even if you just see them—you know, like they're my brother's relatives, but if I just happen to see them—you're just glad to see them even if you don't talk to them as often as you would your own family. It starts to get really weird, you know, when your stepfather is divorced from your mom. And he's married again and I know his wife and she's really great. He has a way of marrying really neat women. I like all the women that he's married. It's neat. A positive.

JILL, Age 28

35

Work on Forgiving Your Parents for Being Human

Forgiveness is the act of admitting we are like other people.

—CHRISTINA BALDWIN

Parents don't normally do things purposely to hurt their kids. But, of course, a lot of things they do, especially when everyone is in the middle of a divorce, can hurt you a lot.

It won't be helpful to pretend that nothing can hurt you or to try to hide out from having anything to do with your family just because being around them is painful a lot of the time. The best way to get over feeling hurt is to begin by accepting the fact that you *do* hurt. Then you can move on from there to try to find ways to help yourself feel better.

If your father is grouchy, don't pick a fight with him or try to cheer him up with joking around or being extra cheerful yourself. Try telling him that you notice he's really grouchy. Then let him have some space to work it out.

If your mother forgets a special date she's made with you to pick you up at school or to go to some event together, let her know that you wish she had remembered. But don't write it off; don't tell yourself you'll never rely on *her* again. Give her a chance to improve.

Both parts of this advice are important: First, pay attention to what's making you feel bad. Then try to forgive your parents for the mistakes they make and the bad moods they're in.

Some parents go through a bad period during a divorce when they are so distracted by their own feelings of sadness, fear, and anger that they are not able to attend to their kids as well as they should. Usually they come out of that stage within a few months. Other parents never seem able to give you what you most need from them. They suddenly reveal sides of themselves that you never saw while they were married. Try to be realistic about your parents' individual strengths and weaknesses. Be proud of their strengths. Try to forgive them for their weaknesses or just for being different from what you thought they were. You'll be able to get more out of your relationship with them that way than if you just stay angry, resentful, or feel sorry for yourself.

- Pay attention to what's working and not working in your relationship with each of your parents.

- Let your parents know how you feel about their behavior—as calmly as you can.

- Give them a chance.

You learn no one is perfect. Your parents are the first people you know. Naturally, you think they have no problems and are mature, etcetera. So when these idealistic visions are broken, you learn for the first time that all people have faults. Only now am I able to see my mother and dad as people, not untouchable, perfect people that I could not understand or relate to. I never really thought much about the two of them. I never looked to see what of them was inside of me. When I was in high school and my parents were separating, I started to notice that my father treated my mother with a wicked silence, or spoke to her as though every word that she said was idiotic. They were just so miserable together. They do better apart.

LAURA, Age 22

So I'm living with my dad alone and it's kind of just dad and son, still seeing my mom on the weekends. Then he starts bringing around this guy all the time who was real effeminate. And when I met this guy, I was old enough that I could see he was effeminate. A friend of mine would come over and we would laugh about him. And then, it was like a month, he was coming over every weekend. And I didn't think anything of it, you know I thought he was just a friend. I told my mom, there's this guy, he's always coming over. He acts kind of effeminate. And my mom said, "I can't believe he's doing this." She told me, "You know, your father's gay." I didn't believe it. I cried and then I didn't believe it. The guy continued to live there. At first he was living upstairs, but then he gradually started to be sleeping with my father. And I was like, fine, this is your thing, but this isn't a natural environment for me. I need to be with a regular mom and pop. And he couldn't understand that. I said, "I need to be with a normal situation. This isn't healthy." I was going through puberty at the time. . . . You know, when you're that young, you just get excited over anything. It was like a really scary thing. . . . I live in another state with my mother now. I haven't visited my father in about a year or maybe two. It's just too much. I'm not really ready for it, I'm always in a way putting it off. They're not real weirdos or a type. They, I guess you could say pretty much they're in love. I never really understood that they could be in love, but now I understand that it's a real love. It was really different though.

JOSH, Age 18

36

Try Not to Let Yourself Get Stuck with Bitter Feelings

When one door of happiness closes, another opens; but often we look so long at the closed door that we do not see the one which has been opened for us.

—HELEN KELLER

Easier said than done. Strange things are happening in your life and there's not a whole lot you can do about it. You can try to adjust, try to be as understanding as possible, try not to take things too personally, but you are probably not going to feel too positive about the whole situation.

In some cases, people don't seem to have too big a problem adjusting to all of the stuff that is happening to them, but most of us agonize over it. You may feel messed with, you may feel betrayed, you could feel abandoned, moved around like a pawn, unloved, isolated, depressed, or any other of a whole range of emotions. You may be just fine. Sometimes you are going to hurt.

Holding a grudge is not in the best interest of anyone. It is not good for you because it keeps you from getting on with your life and enjoying other things. It is a waste of your time to dwell on the things that have made you feel bad in the past. Bitterness is natural, but you can't move on with your life if you are stuck feeling bad about something that you can't control.

Sure, unpleasant things have probably happened in your family since this whole thing started. Okay, your father is insensitive or your mother can be a shrew. They have made mistakes; maybe they never did get a good grip on that temper, or your father had an affair, or your mother ran off for a month. If you can't let it go, if you can't move on and try to build a relationship based more on what's happening now than what they did then, you are not doing yourself any favors.

None of this is to say that you should just forgive and forget every horrible thing that has happened, but don't make a habit out of dwelling on it to the exclusion of all else. You are the only person who can have any say about what is going on in your own head. If you want to spend the rest of your life obsessing about the things that your parents have done, feel free. But you will probably be happier if you can move on.

Forgiveness, while laudable, is not always necessary. No one is expecting you to apply for sainthood or to relinquish every nasty thought that skitters across your mind. You don't have to feel okay about the things that have happened, you don't have to be wildly ecstatic about the mistakes that your parents have made. You don't have to approve or anything. You just have to do the best thing for you and not make a whole life out of feeling bad about the things that other people have done.

It is much easier to sit here and tell you not to hold on to your bitterness than it is for you to let go of the things that hurt you. It is worth considering though. Part of personal growth is learning what to hold on to and what to let slide. There are probably going to be things that you just can't let go of—at least not yet. Time will help.

- Bitterness serves no purpose other than to make you miserable. You have a lifelong responsibility to yourself not to do things that make you feel any worse than you have to.

- You are not helping out the object of your bitterness at all by dwelling on it. You're not fixing anything.

- Easier said than done, giving up a grudge like that. But, rest assured you're better off without it.

The bitterness I felt was doing me more harm than it was good. When it came down to it, I had to look more at my survival than I did at anything else. So when the anger was tearing me apart I had to let go of it. I can't sit here and say I'm not angry. Sure I'm angry. I think Dad really messed up. And I'm angry for what he's done to my mother. I'm angry for the way he's handling the divorce, but I don't let myself get bitter because there are so many other things in my life that I want to enjoy and if I become bitter it'll take over. And I can't let that happen. I've come to the point where I basically just joke about it because it is almost funny. It's such a hideous situation that it's funny. My mom and I even joke about it a lot, my friends joke with me about it. I feel sorry for my dad. He's done this for a reason. He's the way he is for a reason. His father just drilled into him about his faults. It was sort of the conditional love letter: If you don't do this, you're not worthy. I feel sorry for him.

PAM, Age 19

I came home from school one day when I was in, I guess, fifth grade, and all these big army bags and boxes were on our porch. I was like, "Wow, she finally threw him out." But then he came back while we were away for a couple of days to see my grandmother. We opened the door and saw the kitchen was on fire. My dad apparently was upstairs, but he was stoned and had made some popcorn and there was a big hole in the pot. It had stuck to the electric burner. The whole house was just—he didn't even remember—he was upstairs and the whole kitchen was just . . . My sister, she was about two, she just didn't know what was going on. Then I think it was the next day my mother threw him out. It was kind of weird because I didn't really know him and now I'm still struggling to put that away and try to do something with our relationship. . . . I'm kind of cynical. I had really no childhood. I had so much adult stuff thrust on me. And people say to me, well, get over it now, it's over and done with, and they tell me I should really just keep going, but I'm not happy. I didn't have time to deal with this when I was trying to help my mom over a rough time. But now I'm standing here and I'm dealing with it along with other things that come up.

MARIANNE, Age 25

37

Cut Yourself Some Slack:
A Divorce Takes Years, Not Days,
to Get Through

Time heals griefs and quarrels, for we change and are no longer the same persons.

—BLAISE PASCAL

Clearly a divorce is not something that you are going to be dealing with this week and then never have to think about again. After all, once your parents get divorced, they will always be divorced. Realistically speaking, it may take quite a while to develop efficient coping mechanisms for any event or series of events that is going to affect you for years to come. You are going to come across a lot of things in this whole, big, bad world that don't make you happy. You usually can't just nod your head, mutter something uplifting, and wander off into the sunset feeling alright. It will take you some time to work out how you're feeling before things become familiar enough for you to feel comfortable with them.

People rarely know exactly how to get through things. Rest assured that they end up getting through, over, or past them somehow and wind up stronger, or at least not beaten, on the other side. As Nietzsche said, "What does not kill me makes me stronger." The idea that the things that hurt us the most make us more fit in the future is kind of cool, don't you think? It works, too; once you learn to deal with some really harsh things, the rest of the hard stuff may not seem so bad after all. You just need to accept that things take time, internal change among them. It takes years to reorganize your thoughts and work through the whole barrel of emotional stones that has just been rolled onto your head. Naturally, this may seem crushing!

You really can't rush to relieve yourself of this sudden burden. For one thing, certain kinds of wisdom are not acquired overnight. Take your time, work through how you feel, see how things work out by themselves, and change things that don't work for you. All of these things take the time they take. There is no reason on earth why you have to figure out everything immediately, nor will you be able to.

Have you ever actively taken an inventory of what you're thinking? It only takes a couple of minutes. One day, on your way to school or in the shower, you can take a few minutes to catalog all of the bits in your life that you are trying to work through. People in formation—in other words, the young among us—always have a lot of major life stuff to work through. All people need to take stock once in a while. Blinding insights into your particular situation and quick-fix solutions are unlikely to occur to you while you brush your hair. You will know better what you are thinking and feeling if you deliberately ponder your situation once in a while instead of trying to wish it away.

You may notice changes in your state of mind over time; try to be aware of these. They indicate progress. It isn't necessary to start a regimen of self-help. Things will get better if you just give them time, a bit of attention, and room to improve.

There is no easy or quick way to make yourself feel better when you are adjusting to big changes. If you think you have found a quick escape route, you are wrong. People would spend a lot less time feeling miserable if they could just press a button and change how they feel. We can't. Feelings are messy and unpredictable. You will get through this trouble in time, but time is what it takes.

- Time is on your side. You are not working through this divorce on a deadline. Be gentle.

- Knowing yourself is useful in all kinds of other situations, too.

- Just think how strong you must be already and how much stronger you'll be by the time things become more normal.

I think I was seven when my dad actually left. Then for the next ten years they were arguing about money. So they were separated but they were not really divorced until I was 17 years old, at which point my dad remarried right away. He was with his girlfriend for nine of those ten years. Now my parents get along pretty well. They're still uncomfortable, or my dad will do something like barge into the house. But generally they're pretty good. Like if my mom needs something to be done around the house and she can't do it herself, he's always there to help out. So he's really cool about that. They get along. A little bit uncomfortable at times, but for the most part they're friends, I would say. Looking back, it's really weird, because I can't re-member my dad ever living in the house with my mom and I. I think it's kind of cool in a way, I'm happy with it now, the divorce. I mean at first, when they initially told me, I cried and I was really upset, but a lot of people had harder times than I did. It was pretty easy compared to some.

DONNA, Age 20

My dad moved out in April of my sophomore year. I was 16. They had arguments before, but I didn't know that it was a big problem. I was totally shocked and surprised, I didn't know what was going on at all. My mom was, too, my mom didn't know that there were any problems, at least when I talked to her about it. And he moved in with this woman so I guess he'd had an affair, although he denies it. Now they broke up and he lives in an apartment and I don't talk to him that much. But he does my taxes and he gave me a ride back to school and he sends me National Geographic *and money. Mom and Dad try to ignore each other, but they have to talk sometimes because they've got kids in common. But they're getting a lot better. In the beginning they got along until my mom realized what hap-pened because she was in shock. Then she got completely angry, but now it's better because she got the house and she's happy about that . . . and she's got a boyfriend, and that's good. My parents get along, but only when they have to.*

ERICA, Age 19

38

Some Parents Make It Especially Difficult to Work Things Out with Them

Can't nobody solve the problem but the person hisself.
—HERBERT SINGLETON

The truth of the matter, as you have probably already noticed, is that people aren't perfect. If your parents were perfect, they wouldn't be getting divorced. They would be blissfully living the American dream (it's called a dream for a reason, campers), and they would be mind-bogglingly dull. Sure, this kind of drama in your life isn't always fun. Yeah, okay, you could do without the screaming fights, the money worries, the legal baloney, and the split loyalties, but think how interesting it all is. At least it isn't dull.

Since your parents are clearly not perfect (who is?), there is always the possibility that you won't get along with them. There is supposed to be a kind of lifelong loyalty and devotion

174

to the people who brought you into this world, but there are times and situations where it is just plain unhealthy to be dealing with them.

If your folks are doing you more harm than good, if you have a truly dysfunctional relationship with one of your parents, it is in your best interest to try to work it out. Your parents certainly have problems of their own that have little to do with you, and it tends, for the most part, not to be a good idea to totally sever relations with your relations unless it is absolutely unavoidable and in the best interest of all concerned.

The fact of the matter is that it is going to be especially hard to give up on a parent who you live with. This is probably a good thing. You need them and they probably need you during this difficult time. Also, by the time you are free of custodial obligations as dictated by a court of law, you will probably also be old enough to know what is really best for you. You may have gained a better understanding of your parents as people rather than authority figures.

Your parents have problems. All people do. You have them, too, and they are not all to be blamed on your folks. If you have not been living with your mother for several years, you probably don't know each other as well as you'd like. You may be growing more apart as time goes on, and you may be finding it more and more difficult to get along with her. This is not about curfews or taking out the trash; if you two are totally incompatible as human beings, as mother and child, you may have to rethink the relationship in terms of what you need versus what your parent can give.

Alas, there are times when there is nothing you can do. You can't force your parents to change for the sake of your relationship. Give them time, give them space, make some changes yourself. But if that isn't the answer, you just may have to get away from the relationship.

Parents have been making their children miserable for centuries. It is a fact of life. Sometimes it gets out of hand and it is in the best interest of everyone involved to get out of the situation, put a stop to the destructive relationship. Some parents are very damaged people. It's sad if you have drawn the ticket for one of those. But if someone is clearly doing you harm, you must protect yourself from that person, even if it is your mother or father.

This is definitely a situation that calls for consulting a trustworthy adult, preferably a trained counselor. You may need help in figuring out the difference between not seeing eye to eye and really being harmed by a parent who is physically or emotionally abusive. Some of us want to give up on our relationships with our parents, particularly ornery parents, too quickly. But others stick it out too long and hurt themselves more by allowing their parent to go on hurting them. It's crucial for you to be clear about what's really going on. *Get help* with this one!

Unless you are absolutely positive that your relationship with one of your parents (or worse, both of them) cannot be salvaged now and must be abandoned, don't do anything drastic. You can't hold on to false hope—that things are just going to work out in the end—but you also can't just walk away from the person who made half of you. It's bound to hurt.

This is one of the toughest issues in this book. We don't have any foolproof advice for you, either, except use your head, think things through (with help from someone wise, if possible), and proceed with caution. Be certain of what you need to do before you do anything.

- You may find it impossible to ever get along with one of your parents. This is not unheard of and it is nobody's fault.

- People are different, and this is a time of major change for your parents. Things are going to be tense; give it time but know your limits.

- Ask yourself if it is going to hurt more to keep working on your relationship or to let it go. Be sure of your answer before acting on it.

My father's very calm and inward. But he was hurt, of course, he loves her. He's getting over it now, but he loved my mother and she broke his heart. The worst thing was when my father went away to Las Vegas after they had separated and my mother was supposed to come by our house and make sure I was all right. The night he was supposed to come back I was awakened in the middle of the night by yelling and screaming— my father in a rage. My mother had come while I was asleep, which was after two a.m., and was sleeping with this man she was having an affair with in my parents' bed. She claims my father told her he was coming the next day, but in any case that's just a sick thing to do. I had so many angry feelings toward my mother. I didn't realize that at first. My mother would say, "Don't lay a guilt trip on me. I've never had my own life. I admit I'm a lousy mother and I just want my own life for myself now." What a great thing to say to your children!

KIMBERLY, Age 21

I haven't visited my father in about a year or maybe two. It's just too much. I'm not really ready for it; I'm always in a way putting it off. The thing that bothers me is that whenever he writes me I'm like kind of something of his past. Everything's like, since he's a businessman his life kind of revolves around business. He writes everything like a business. I don't feel like

I have much of a relationship with my father now. He's become like a figurehead. He's just like—he doesn't have anybody besides his lover and me. He just goes to work and comes home. He has a lot of money and stuff, but that's all he has. And I just don't look up to him at all. Whenever I'd ask him about things he'd just tell me very superficial stuff that I didn't think was very important. I feel like I know more about life than he does. I'm somewhat dependent on my father financially for college and it's kind of hard because you have to be a little bit hypocritical. Sometimes you don't feel like calling him, but you call him because you know that you have to just to make sure that the tuition gets paid. I don't see it as going both ways, because he doesn't really care anymore. I'm a part of his past now. He's at the point where he knows what he wants with his life. He's doing what he wants with his life, and he doesn't really want anything to do with being a heterosexual at all. Being a parent is not the fun that it used to be. It wasn't really that he was gay, but just the fact that he's very selfish. It's my needs, my needs. He's a very selfish person.

JOSH, Age 18

39

It Gets Better, But It's Never Over

I do not think I will ever reach a stage when I will say, "This is what I believe. Finished." What I believe is alive . . . and open to growth.

—MADELEINE L'ENGLE

You have read and been told over and over that you still have two parents no matter what they do. This is a fact of nature, and whether you like it or not, unless you go to some pretty severe criminal or biochemical extremes, you will continue to have two parents for a good long time.

Two people who have children in common can never really be totally disassociated from each other. You yourself are a constant reminder that they once shared their life with someone who's not around anymore. Parents are never really, totally divorced. They just can't be as long as they have kids. So even though things usually smooth out and get more comfortable and familiar as time goes on, it is never totally over.

Maybe you will have two separate parental visits while you are at college, because they can't visit together anymore. Maybe

179

you have to send the wedding invitations to several addresses just to include your immediate family. Maybe you won't know where to take your own kids for their first Christmas. There are always going to be little things to grapple with that have no traditional, prescribed, tried-and-true, normal responses in your particular situation.

In any event, there never will come a time when your parents are totally back the way they were (probably for the best). For a long while, unless both your parents immediately re-marry and stay stable in that marriage forever, things will be changing pretty constantly. Actually, that whole change thing is not so bad. There is no progress without change, you know. A life that always stays the same is not really worth bothering with after a while.

You will indubitably, over time and after lots of blood, sweat, and tears, get used to your personal situation. Yes, it is true, this could happen to you. As long as you are the child of your parents, you are going to have this divorce thing as part of your resumé. Fact is, you just can't get away. You can get over the shock, you can get your life moving along a bit more normally, you can, indeed, get used to almost anything— certainly more than you think you can. It gets better as you get used to it.

At first it might seem totally awkward to visit your father across town in that strange apartment. It could seem completely wrong to have your mother dating. With time and understanding, these things will cause you a bit less trauma every time they occur. You may end up enjoying the fact that you have two distinct places you can call home. Acclimation is an important part of what you are going through. When things settle down they will probably freak you out and piss you off less, but they will never be static or completely over and done with.

- Divorce doesn't end. Legal proceedings end, but once they are over, you are always part of a divorced family.

- You will eventually get used to some of the things that currently bother you.

- Things get easier as they surprise you less.

I think my parents' divorce is a major thing in my not getting along with my father, because I didn't live with him. He just doesn't know me like a father would. My sister, I always look at their relationship and think, what if it had been me? And oftentimes I was glad it wasn't because of certain ways that he is, but it's too bad. And he really regrets it. He always has said, when we have these big heart-to-heart talks, it always comes back to that he feels really bad that their marriage ended up like it did. He thinks that I was cheated. And I always feel bad for wanting to say, "It hasn't been that bad for me except for us. You're the one that is still carrying around a lot of stuff. Not me. My life is fine except that we can't talk to each other." I'm not really close to his family and he really resents that. My sister, I really envy her. She's a totally different kind of personality from my father or me. She's really bubbly and outgoing. If they're having a problem she wants to know what she can do to take care of it. She says, "Dad, what's wrong? Sorry, whatever it was let's just talk about it." And she is able to— he eventually comes around, and she is able to deal with him. You have to learn how to deal with him and I can't, I don't.

JILL, Age 28

My parents have good communication. They talk occasionally because there are a lot of things that go on that require their attention. When I became a diabetic two years ago, they proba-

bly would have had to communicate a lot. Now they have a problem with my brother and they're always talking about what he should do. I think my parents probably feel there will always be problems. I've had monetary problems and this and that, all kinds of problems. And I can always go to them. It's so funny because I'm 25 now and my dad was 26 when I was born, so I'm pretty much the same age he was when I was born. And still I don't feel like it's me talking to another adult. I've never gotten to that point. You know, I'm an adult and my dad's an adult, and I understand that, but it still feels like I'm talking to my dad. And I'm glad for that. I'm glad that I can talk to my dad about more adult issues now, but I'm still glad that he'll always be a different type of a person in my head than another guy his age, that he'll act like a father toward me.

STEVE, Age 25

40

Your Own Future Belongs to You: Make Plans

The wave of the future is coming and there is no stopping it.

—Anne Morrow Lindbergh

Okay, here it is. Coming right at you. Here's a revelation. It takes two people to make a kid, just like it takes two to tango, only with a lot more time commitment and a nine-month waiting period.

Personal incompatibility almost certainly had quite a lot to do with your folks splitting up. They probably thought that it could work when they got together and had you, but over a period of time they realized that it just wasn't going to work out the way they had hoped. They then decided to separate and, ultimately, to divorce. Whatever it was that made them decide to split had to do with inconsistencies in their behavior, characters, or their expectations of each other and of marriage.

Are we in agreement up to this point? Okay. Here we get

philosophical and pseudoscientific: Human personality is formed by a combination of environmental influences and genetic traits. You are technically made up of relatively equal parts of each of your parents. Physically this is true. One sperm and one egg came together to make the enigmatic and multifaceted being that you are now. These two itty-bitty stupid-looking things worked in combination with your experience of life up to this point to make you what you are today. You are about half Dad and half Mom, with some other things thrown in to make life interesting.

We're almost to the finish line here. It has already been proven that your parents could not live together. They have admitted their incompatibility by moving away from each other. They have tried to recognize their differences and work things out, hopefully with a minimum of pain and suffering for all concerned, by moving on and getting away from each other.

This is not making things easy for you, because these are two halves of your being that are at odds. They clearly are not predisposed to getting along, so you have to figure out how to make your own two halves work together for your best benefit.

This is not a multiple personality argument. You are probably very well blended between your two influences, but their coming apart may have made you feel split down the middle yourself. You probably need a bit of time and thought to bring yourself back into alignment.

Look at how well you've mixed until now and take heart. You will make things work even though your two sponsors didn't. This is your chance to join two unique and different forces together for even greater strength—sort of like making steel. Think of yourself as a collection of the *best* parts of two totally different people. Isn't that a liberating thought?

Get going, you yin-yang, you. You're fire and water, heaven and earth. Use what you were born with to do the best you can. Your script in the past may have been written largely by the adults in your life, but now it's your turn to write your own story. Make it a good one. Congratulations. You are hereby declared a gourmet genetic blend. Do with yourself what you will.

- You have a whole future ahead of you. Just thought it was worth mentioning.

- Make plans for yourself. You are in charge now.

- Remember, you have the combined strength of two opposing human beings. You are powerful!

Some people think it's really strange, but I wouldn't change anything in my life. If I had to do it all over again I'd do it just like that. Because I know what I want out of a man—out of a husband and out of a father. I'm a sensitive person. I really feel like I know I'm caring; I'm a nurturing person, I'm sensitive. And yet I'm really strong and independent. When I was nine I was cooking and cleaning the house and watching my little sister. Because I had to. There was no one else to do it. That's why I've always had friends who were older than me. I've dated older guys because I was my mom's best friend. We still are. She knows everything about me. We have an incredible relationship. And that's what my father hates. I think that's why my sister is his favorite. He always tells me, "You're so much like your mother." And he hates that. But I'm proud of it. I'm proud as hell of it. She worked night and day for us, and because of her I've become independent. I take care of my baby sisters like a mother. I look out for them. I have motherly instincts for them, before they get hurt or after they get hurt. These experiences have made me the kind of person that I am.

My weaknesses and my strengths, what I'm afraid of and what I'm not, what I've seen, what to stay away from. I know what I want now from my life and from the future.

LISA, Age 19

It's not like my dad was ever mean to my mom. My parents were separated and divorced mainly because they just didn't agree on things. They are two very different people and I swear I have the genetic combination of both of them. I go to the store and I buy something because I have the compulsive nature of my mom to buy things or collect things, and I feel bad about it afterward because I have the thriftiness and tightness that my dad has. And I can see how that might have been a real heavy tension between the two.

STEVE, Age 25

41

Expect Some Changes in the Way Your Relatives Treat You

Family is just accident.... They don't mean to get on your nerves. They don't even mean to be your family. They just are.

—MARSHA NORMAN

When your parents get divorced there will be changes beyond who you are living with at any given moment. Your entire family is going through some awkward times and it is going to be difficult for other people who are related to you to adjust to your new circumstances.

Sometimes your relatives start treating you differently—they may act like you are only half related to them now. As if any of that stuff should change! They might feel like some of the family lines have been severed and that they have to choose sides. They may not know that they should act just the way they always have.

They may be wonderful and try to give you a little extra love

187

and attention, because they see you are stuck in the middle of something hard, or they may make things even more difficult for you. It all depends on the kind of people you are related to and on your particular situation.

If you spend most of your time with your mother, you will probably find yourself more distanced from your father's relatives than you used to be. Since you are not all living under the same roof anymore, things like this are bound to change. Where two families had previously been joined by marriage, they are not anymore, and this brings up whole complex emotional, ethical, and social issues that you don't need to deal with. For example, who do you invite to your birthday? To your graduation? To your wedding or whatever? Does it matter where it is?

You should not feel obligated to curb your guest list because your relatives may be uncomfortable with each other. This is their problem, and if they have any beef with whatever you decide to do, they will have to work things out for themselves. They are under no obligation to attend. If you are afraid of your grandparents making a scene around your mother, warn everyone that you will not tolerate it. It really is that simple. These are the people with whom you share genes and chromosomes and stuff; you ought to be able to tell them to behave themselves if you feel the need, and they should respect your wishes.

Sometimes relatives seem to decide that you have been divorced, too, that they are not related to you anymore. This is a really bad idea for all concerned. They lose out on a valuable family asset (you), and you lose a part of your family. And let's face it, no matter how much they may make you wish to deny it, you probably really do love your relatives. You might call them or write to them and let them know that you miss being in touch and would like to remain close to them. If they don't respond with care and sensitivity to your feelings, try to let it go. There are, unfortunately, some people who would rather cut you out of their lives than love you. If so, let them go.

Don't let any of your relatives give you a hard time about being related to anyone on the other side of your family. Feel free to set them straight about how you are descended equally from each side of your family. It doesn't matter how much they dislike your other parent; it is wrong for them to tell you about it. They have no right to make you feel bad about mistakes that your parents have made. That's what they are: mistakes *your parents* made. Your relatives should love you just the same.

Insensitivity among family members is as old as the stars. It should be addressed with honesty. This is another one of those areas where you may feel more adult than the adults and where you have an opportunity to teach *them* a thing or two.

- You are just as related to everyone in your extended family as you ever were.

- Any problem that they have with the other side of your family is their problem. Not yours.

- You may want to give them a chance to come to their senses. They're probably trying their best.

I remember that my father's parents stopped calling the house as soon as my father moved out. We used to see them a couple of times a year, either at home or where they lived. It was always really nice visiting them or having them visit us. That all stopped when Dad moved out, because they couldn't stand my mother. It was like they decided that my brothers and I were my mother's children and that we weren't their grandkids anymore. I didn't see them for about four years after that and then only when they came, just for the day, to my graduation. I saw them for about an hour and it was really strange. It was like they were trying to give me money instead of seeing me, because I was related to "her." It really hurt my mother, too, because she felt like they were taking out all of their stuff on us and it was totally unfair. They just completely closed their ranks; it's like we're not even related anymore except that we used to be. My mother's parents never did anything like that. They still want to see us and everything, in fact they see us more now because they know they're it. They even tried to keep in touch with my father, but he's a lot like his folks and wasn't very good about that. It's this whole big deal. I love them and everything, but I can't stand that they're like this. I feel like I shouldn't mention my mother or our house around them because they'll get all mad or kick me out or something. It's just easier most of the time not to see them, because they're not the easiest people to talk to. I'm not even sure that they remember that they have a granddaughter in college, or if they do know, I don't know if they care.

NORA, Age 20

My father's family always picked us up from the time that we were little. Now it's kind of hard for us because I'm in school, my sister's in school, she's got a child. But we still try to see them. His family helped us, sent money, picked us up, took us on vacations, things he should have been doing. His parents and my aunts and my uncles. They're really nice. They tried to keep in contact with us; they looked at us as if we were family more than not. They're pretty good. I know about them, I know their phone numbers, I know where they live, whereas him, he won't even tell us. I think it might have to do with his wife, though, because we don't get along with her.

RONNIE, Age 22

42

Your Parents May Wind Up Happier Than They Were Before

She seems to have had the ability to stand firmly on the rock of her past while living completely and unregretfully in the present.

—MADELEINE L'ENGLE

Well, they did get divorced because they weren't happy with the way things were going, didn't they? Yeah, things get tough while they try to work out their new life-styles. You are all going to have to work out your new relationships with each other and probably face the addition of more people to the family. But once everything settles down, they *should* be at least as happy, if not more so, as they were before the divorce.

Happy parents make everyone's life much easier, yours included. It is not a betrayal of your family if your folks decide they enjoy not being married; it ought to be a welcome development. As long as they are not going to be together, they might as well be happy about it. Surely it is a great relief for them to find that they are capable of being happy after all they've been through.

When your parents are feeling good about themselves and the way that their lives are working out, they are going to be able to be better parents. Miserable people are not so good at recognizing the needs of their children; that's just how it works. If they are feeling better off, relieved, or just plain cheerful, they will have much more to give you in the usual and even the extraordinary parenting way.

Often one parent is a lot happier postdivorce than the other parent. (This may be more evidence of their being very different people.) If your father is still angry at your mother while she is whistling a happy tune and skipping along spreading sunshine, you may feel torn between them. This is normal. It is pretty common, if unproductive, for one parent to hold a grudge, and it is normal for you to feel a mite strange about it.

When it is clear to your folks that the end of the world is not coming because they broke it off, when they are feeling secure in their new lives and stuff like that, they'll probably be more open to feeling good about how things are working out. You can't really expect everyone to be jumping for joy right off the bat, but it is also not good for them to brood too long over the problems with their marriage once it has ended. It would even be okay for you to let them know that you'd like to see them happy and that there's no time like the present to begin to work on making things more pleasant and satisfying for themselves.

Be glad they are happy. It means the worst is over. It's likely to be an up and down kind of thing, though. With so much changing in their lives, they are liable to have days that knock them flat just when they've been kicking up their heels at long last. They could be working really hard, having trouble meeting payments, still be in court in some ugly battle or another, or maybe having problems in other parts of their lives and still be feeling better about the future, about you, about themselves or about any old random thing. But even if *everything* is not coming up roses, the fact that some things are looking up shows that there is room and the possibility for even more improvement.

Whatever the circumstances, your parents must be feeling some relief from at least one megastress: the difficulty of admitting that their marriage has failed. Now that they are moving on into the future, they have every reason to be feeling good. In the long run, we'll all keep our fingers crossed that they end up a lot happier than they've been, so that this long, tough trip will have been worth it. For all of you.

- It might not happen immediately, but it is more than likely that your parents will end up happier than they were when they were in a nonworking marriage.

- Happy parents are better parents. They are also a whole lot more fun to be around than sulking, depressed, fatalistic parents.

- If they were unhappy enough to get divorced in the first place, then they darn well better be happier when it is all over and done with.

I always felt that my mom was really strong only because of the fact that she was able to raise two kids on her own. She worked very hard. There were situations where I have vague memories of someone trying to break in one time and she just called the cops. It wasn't like it scared her or anything. She had several different relationships and I was usually not happy with most of them. She got married again one time. I had a *stepfather and five stepsisters and we had big problems with all of that. He eventually died in a car crash while they were married, which was too bad. . . . They were together for about two years and then he died. I guess my mom started then to work at the Post Office. . . . So there were times when I hardly ever saw my mom and we had to pretty much take care of ourselves. But she never quit. She just had her tenth anniversary there, even though she has medical problems. She's getting $18 an hour or something like that. It's hard to beat that at all, doing receptionist type stuff. Like I said, she never quit. She finally got together with a guy named Charles and she's still with him and this was about five or six years ago. At first I didn't care for him, but now I've grown to accept him. He's almost like a second father figure, much more than my stepfather ever was, because he's a very kind guy. He's just a nice guy and he's got very strict ways he thinks things should be done, but he's kind of a loose kind of person. He's a really nice guy. He was a Vietnam vet. They met when my mom was getting into birds. She raises birds, and they still do that. I'm glad she found someone like Charles after some not good relationships. He can help her out.*

STEVE, Age 25

My relationship with my mother is so strong, it's so wonderful. She's my best friend. And she has grown into a totally different person. She was really depressed with my dad. She was always really depressed. It kind of took the bottom falling out for her to climb out of that depression. And now she's got a lot of problems with her business and stuff, but she's really happy, and so when the two of us get together we just laugh and we're really understanding, really open and close.

PAM, Age 19

43

Face Facts: Most Divorces Create Money Problems

Money is only money, beans tonight and steak tomorrow.
So long as you can look yourself in the eye.

—MERIDEL LE SUEUR

Okay, your family has been living at a certain standard for a while now. Whatever that standard is for your family, be it a lot or a little, it has probably been based on how much money your folks make together in a given amount of time. When the household separates, the same amount of money has to cover more stuff. When one of your folks moves out, there are new expenses. Now they both have rent and/or mortgage expenses. They both have legal expenses.

The division of money, financial responsibilities, and property can also be the major issue or argument in their settlement. Dad may think that he needs more money than Mom is willing to give to feed and clothe the kids. One of them may feel he or she is being treated unfairly, that the other one is getting more than they deserve.

In some ways this is kind of reasonable. Hold up, keep reading, bear with this for a minute. Dad works hard for his money. When he lived with the rest of his family, he could see how his hard-earned dollars were being spent for the welfare of his family. Now that he (or Mom, as the case may be) is living somewhere else, he may feel like his money is going to care for someone that he can't live with anymore. This doesn't mean that he doesn't love his kids, but it makes him uncomfortable. It also may be that he doesn't feel he can afford to keep his family living at the same level as before, what with all the added expenses of divorce.

Chances are that your folks aren't really getting along very well. They are trying to live apart. They are probably carefully considering the cost of things they used to be able to pay for without blinking. It's not easy for them to adjust to having less, any more than it is for you. And they probably feel a little guilty about it, too. You can be sure that most parents are trying, though. Most parents really want to do the best they can for both themselves and their kids.

It doesn't seem fair that just when everybody needs a vacation the most, they suddenly can't afford one. Your folks don't want to cut out vacations, or skimp on holidays and birthdays any more than you want them to. Divorces are so expensive emotionally that it seems especially harsh for them to cost so much money on top of it all.

If you want more for yourself, you may have to face up to the fact that it will require you to provide for yourself in some ways. You may have to get out there and find a part-time job so you have enough money to keep up with what you want to do. You may have to do more than you're used to doing for yourself, but that can be good for you, too. Builds character, they'll probably tell you. This doesn't mean you will always enjoy it, but it is another way that you will be able to learn about how the world works.

Because of your family's current situation, you may have to move out of your home into one that is more affordable. This is really common. Lots of divorces are marked by moving. Hey, you may move into a neighborhood that you like better, or you may get a room with a view this time. Even if you really, really hate the idea of moving, you might as well look for what may be positive about it.

Money problems aren't fun for anyone. They are kind of inevitable, though, when all of your family's assets are being divided up in the name of justice. If your family doesn't have money problems when your parents get divorced, you are in the minority. If they do have problems making ends meet, just know that it is to be expected and that things will probably improve with time as your parents get used to new arrangements and distribution of their funds.

- It is to be expected that when the same amount of money is divided up between two separate households that things will be tight for a while. Try not to feel let down.

- Money situations will probably improve once your parents get used to their new expenses and make whatever adjustments are needed to make ends meet.

- Any changes in life-style coming from money problems should be taken as lightly as possible. It is love, not material gifts or other stuff, that makes a family work.

There's a lot of financial confusion. My father has a job and owns a store. He always says he's broke and he doesn't have the money to pay the phone bill at the store or the electric bill.

Then he tells me that he wants to buy me a new car stereo. Just pay the electric bill! It's really hard for my mom to pay for school, the house, the car and get no help from my father whatsoever except for x dollars a month. There's just something missing. I don't know. So financial stuff has been kind of tight. My mom pays my tuition, room, and board at college, and I pay for everything else. I mean for me. I bought my own car. I think these responsibilities have been good for me, too.

REBECCA, Age 20

With my mother I guess is home, but being away from the rest of my family it was just so weird because I'd be like, "Damn, I need money." And then you look up and you see your mom struggling. It's real different. I guess that could be a hint. Teach the kids not to be so materialistic. Because as long as your parents love you, you can get anything you want. It'll just take a little bit more time. I just saw my mom crying and times were hard because money was low and I just had to be there for her.

ROB, Age 20

Our life is good, but we have financial problems that we have to deal with all the time. The age differences of all us kids add to that. I'm becoming a young woman now and I have some needs. My sister is just 13 and of course she's on the phone all the time and needs a new outfit all the time, needs new jewelry. I went through that. The babies need a pack of diapers every week and a half, need formula. So it's really hard for us. We lived in a three-bedroom apartment, but we just can't do it. There's four kids and two parents. So we moved into a town house, which we're renting, and it's hard to keep up with our rent and utilities. We've cut back on so many things, but still there's always something. We always have some kind of emergency.

LISA, Age 19

44

It Might Be Hard to Cope with School for a While

As we do at such times, I turned on my automatic pilot and went through the motions of normalcy on the outside, so that I could concentrate all my powers on surviving the near-mortal wound inside.

—SONIA JOHNSON

As with any major change in situation or life-style, some areas of your life will be affected by your parents' divorce even when you think they should not be. There is no good time for your parents to split up, but no matter when it happens, it will seem like an especially bad time for it to happen.

Your performance at school may easily be affected by anything upsetting that goes on in your life. Naturally, the divorce of your parents ranks at the top of the list of big upsets. No doubt, no matter how calm you appear on the surface, you are going through a lot of emotional stuff and all kinds of strangeness at home. Since divorce alters your entire home life, your feelings of confusion and upheaval will not pass quickly or be restricted to certain days of the week. You are in the middle of what will be long-lasting alterations to the way you feel and the way you do things. It is good to understand that when your entire life is in flux, distraction is normal and to be expected.

Such a major life-style change will affect your attention and performance at school. If you get into a big fight with one of your friends you will probably not be paying the best sort of attention in history class that day. A divorce in your family has pretty much the same effect. It is one big, long-term, strange thing that can very easily distract you from school. So a lot of kids find that their parents' divorce shows up on their report cards.

Your grades may drop significantly, but this should not make you decide that you are now destined to be a lousy student. Don't use your parents' divorce as an excuse to start slacking. Just keep doing your best. As things calm down, your grades will get back to normal.

Aside from your grades, school is an intensely social environment and you might find that you are feeling kind of uncomfortable just hanging around the way that you used to, or that you are not as interested in the activities that you loved before. Like it or not, you are being compelled to change, and it's happening quickly. Changes in your interests and compatibility with others are a logical consequence.

You can count on being kind of confused about a lot more than just what is going on at home for a while. Once you are used to how your home life is shaping up, school life and your academic performance should even out as well.

Don't make the mistake of blaming your parents for all your troubles. Your life is yours. It doesn't always go smoothly. Everybody gets stuff handed to them that they'd rather not have to accept. But if you don't accept it, you just stay stuck. And everybody knows that the teen years are a real roller coaster ride on the path to self-definition, even for people with utterly stable home lives. If you want help getting your school life back in order, good for you. Seek out the help that you need. Talk to a teacher who has a grip on things or to some other adult you trust.

It can be hard to go on with the same daily routine in one half of your life and to have things totally screwed up in the other. It is also impossible to completely separate your school demeanor from your home one. The feelings that you are going through, the confusion that you feel, will show up in your schoolwork and your school relationships. How could it be otherwise? You are the same person, at home or at school, so how can you totally separate the two? At the same time, you might find that school is kind of a refuge from your rocky home life. It may feel good to get out of the house and into some familiar routines, even if you can't concentrate as well as you usually do.

- Your parents' divorce will probably show up on your report card. If this happens, you are not the first.

- Your attention span might be the first thing to go. You are probably working through some complex issues, and that can be very distracting.

- Try to be aware of your moods and do positive things to keep yourself from flipping out. You will be better able to take care of yourself if you are honest with yourself about what you are going through.

I remember back when I made myself think I didn't care. I'd say to myself, I'm just not going to even worry about it. I'm not going to think about it. My mom said that my teachers in school told her that I would just sit there and space out. I'd just draw all over my papers. When I was in middle school and high school, I couldn't hang around with a lot of people because I didn't feel like I connected with people. I couldn't get into that, because I'd be thinking about weird things. I was probably too analytical of myself. I felt separate from other people, because that was right in the beginning stages of my parents' separation, when I was in fifth and sixth grade. When I went to middle school, I didn't relate to anybody. Some of them were from some hard-core neighborhoods, so I got messed with a lot. I learned how to get along, I hung out with some of those kids, but I couldn't really talk to anyone.

CHARLIE, Age 21

I went to counseling, to lots of different places, from like third grade until tenth grade. Finally I didn't want to do it anymore. It's just bullshit. It wasn't working, obviously. Everyone's life was getting worse and worse and worse. I said, save your money. Go do something else. Then I got into drugs. I tried just about everything. I didn't do any heroin or anything like that. I'd done a lot of LSD, PCP stuff, smoked a lot of pot, did a lot of drinking, and like did coke a couple of times. My brother started in, I guess, because it was something he could see me doing, and like I never thought I had all these friends in high school, but he went into the high school and it was like, "Oh, yeah, you're Tim's brother. I used to hang out with him." Where'd they all come from? He was like, "Everyone knows who you were." So he was gone, taking it 500 yards down the road farther than I had. I look at my dad, my brother, and me and I hope my brother will wake up. I've lost friends; my friend Kenny down in L.A. blew his brains out, he just couldn't take it anymore. And I've had friends just completely burn them-selves out. From when I was about 17½ to when I was 19, I was just like phased out. And then when I was 19 my brother OD'd for like the second time. I looked at it a lot. His life was always like a year ahead of me, like what he'd done. And I was at a point where he had been the year before. I had just about tried everything, and a lot of the stuff just wasn't working anymore. And I started thinking that with all the chemicals that were in my body I was going to get to be where my brother was and I was going to OD. Or I'd have a horrible, miserable life until I was like 40, like my father. Neither one of those options was something I wanted to do. So I decided I'd quit. A friend of my father's took me to an A.A. meeting. I kept going to meetings once or twice a week when I moved up here. Actu-ally, I haven't been to any meetings in a while because my life is so full now. But I keep up on it. [Tim got his GED and has been sober for three years. He is now in college.]

TIM, Age 22

45

Don't Try to Tough It Out:
Ask for Help When You Need It

Whatever you may be sure of, be sure of this: that you are dreadfully like other people.

—James Russell Lowell

Bad things happen all the time. Just because divorce is common does not mean that it doesn't hurt or that you should know what to do. Just because lots of other people have gone through it doesn't make it any easier for you, especially since every divorce, like every family, like every adorable little snowflake, is different.

You are going to have things to deal with that even your friends and acquaintances from divorced families didn't have. And they had some problems that you won't have. This is your life; you're going through a trauma. It is a big deal, but it is not the end of the world. And you shouldn't have to get yourself through it alone.

There are all kinds of reasons you might need outside help.

Most people just feel better when they can talk things over. One approach is talking it out with a good friend. But if you need more in-depth understanding than your friends can give, ask for professional help. It is not any kind of failure to seek out the help of others. It is part of being human. We are a cooperative species. We do best in tribes, with leaders, sooth-sayers, and wise old crones to help us figure things out.

If you had been in a car accident you would go to a doctor. Well, you have been in a car accident of the psyche. It's not necessarily fatal or permanently debilitating, but you ought to get the help you need to get better. You will also not look at this metaphorical road the same way again. There are hazards inherent in being human and having human relationships and you have just been involved in one of them. Pull over, take stock, and figure out if you need help. Don't be afraid, there are probably more people in counseling of some kind or another than there are people who aren't. It's also a safe bet that the ones who are getting the help they feel they need are better off for it.

Help doesn't have to be expensive. Most schools have services for their students that are confidential and cheap (if not free). There are also other ways to find a kind of help that is suitable to you. School counselors may know of community services in your area. Ministers, priests, and rabbis also do counseling or can refer you to people who can help.

Make sure you like and trust the person you end up talking to. Remember, if you don't feel right, if you don't think that a particular situation can work for you, then it can't. If you don't feel comfortable, then it isn't going to do you any good and you might as well not even bother. Get a referral to someone else and try again.

You've probably got issues in your life that could use a good threshing out other than those related to your parents' divorce.

The divorce may be just one thing in the great confusion of life. The help you get doesn't have to focus solely on the divorce. It should be focused on *you*, the things you are concerned about, the things that are causing you pain. Divorce is often the final straw that makes people seek outside assistance in their lives. Yeah, it's a really big straw, but it isn't the whole bale of hay or anything. Hey, there are people who just use the divorce as an excuse to get the help that they have needed for quite some time! Whatever works. Just don't kid yourself.

There are people who never need or want help getting through a tough time. They are not strange or better, just different. If you feel okay with how things are going, or even if you don't and you can handle it alone, bravo. But knowing when you need some help and getting it deserves just as much credit and as many bonus points as knowing that you're okay. Everyone has his or her unique way of going about things; there's nothing wrong with any particular method. But if you are tempted to help yourself feel better by doing a lot of drugs, drinking yourself into a stupor, or driving real fast on a dark, curving road, you are not coping at all. Get help now.

You know your situation and your state of mind better than anyone. Once again, you will have to act like an adult and decide for yourself what will work best for you. No one else can do that for you. If you don't want help, if you don't want to talk, and you're not ready to listen, it isn't going to do you any good to get help, and any good, honest therapist will tell you the same thing.

- If it ain't broke, don't fix it. But if it is broke or even just kind of shaky, get some help before it gets really bad.

- If you decide that you do need help, know that you are the only person who can choose the right person and the right situation to help you. No one else knows exactly what is going on in your head. The therapist who was great for your best friend may or may not be great for you.

- You don't have to be totally overwhelmed by your problems to ask that some attention be paid to them. Your family's divorce is only part of the larger picture of your life, so take a look at all of it while you're at it.

Talking with my friends in junior high, just sharing, commiserating over our home lives helped. I guess my friends are probably the most important people to me, the people I talk to on a regular basis. I could never have made it without my friends. When I was in high school I had this best friend and I would always tell her about my family and how strange it was, and it was very hard to describe why it was so difficult because they weren't hitting each other, they weren't hitting me, it was just strange, sort of subtle warfare—constant. After high school, a couple years ago she came to my house and she saw an interaction go on between me and my mother, and when we left she said, "Now I know what you were talking about. Now I know exactly—before I thought you were exaggerating, but now I see." And when she said that, it just made me feel less crazy. Because it was so impossible to explain. You couldn't say, look, here, see my bruise? It was all mental. Without friendship, the support, or even just commiserating—I'd be lost.

LAURA, Age 22

Talking with my parents about the past is very difficult. They both tend to be very closed people because of the families they came from. If anything's wrong you just go off into another room and don't tell anyone about it. We're a very closed-off family. Some of the counseling I had was helpful, and some of it wasn't. When I was younger and went to a child psychologist it was just playing games and I guess things came out from my actions. Not everything I've been to shrinks for has been the fault of the divorce. I have some of my own problems. I went to another psychologist for a couple of years whom I really hated and that didn't help very much. The one I still see occasionally really listened to me and actually agreed with me from time to time when she thought I was right, I thought I was right, my mother thought I was wrong. I finally had an advocate. It was good. She could say, "You know, you're right, your mother is being a little heavy-handed, she does need to let you have a little more freedom. . . ." I've only recently started figuring out what problems were caused by the divorce. When I started out, I was a little hellion in school. I wouldn't do my work. I got thrown out of class frequently. I was brilliant compared to the rest of the other kids. I understood the work, I just didn't have much patience for it. I'd get in fights. I was eventually transferred into an emotionally impaired classroom. It was very helpful, but it makes you a pariah. That was tough for elementary school. I didn't have very many friends in elementary school. The one friend I did make there is still my very close friend. I've always had a problem with school, with getting it done. Everyone says, "Oh, you test so high, you're so smart," but I can't get things done. That doesn't have anything to do with the divorce. It never came into that. I've only started thinking about the divorce recently.

JOHN, Age 19

46

Keep Those Good Memories of Your Old Family Life

It is not that I belong to the past, but the past that belongs to me.

—MARY ANTIN

Keep your memories? No kidding. What are you supposed to do? Become totally amnesiac about all the years before your parents split up?

If there's one thing we've learned, it's that things in the past don't change. You may wish that you could forget or rewrite the bad times, but they are going to stick with you. Sorry, but it's true. Everything that has ever happened to you has had something to do with making you the complex person that you are today. When bad memories begin to wear you down, you ought to do your best to summon the memories that you like to recall and keep in mind that life just isn't all that bad.

Some people block out unhappy experiences or parts of their lives that are painful to remember. Others dwell on every bad thing that ever happened to them. They appear to thrive on reliving the pain. Neither of these approaches is healthy.

Life is a mixture of good and bad, up and down, happiness and misery. It's probably healthiest for us to make more of the good things than of the miserable things, or at least to keep them in balance.

Remember that good things happen in the strangest of circumstances. Your old family life may have been a really horrible scene, but you can't possibly pretend that it never happened. And why pretend that you don't miss the good times?

Let's say that your whole family—grandparents, aunts and uncles, cousins, whatever, used to have dinner together once a week and you miss that. Feel free to miss it all you want and to look back on it fondly. Life moves everyone away from what is past, whether or not there's been a divorce. We all grow up and away.

Just don't let missing the old stuff get in the way of letting you experience the new stuff. Don't get stuck in a pattern that impedes your progression into the future. This, too, goes for everyone, not just people dealing with a divorce.

Having fun thinking about the past does not necessarily mean that you want things back the way they were. You can miss the past and still appreciate what you have in the present and what you are looking forward to in the future. Having accepted that the past is the past helps you to feel free to reminisce without feeling guilty or sorry for yourself.

- Feeling good about your past should not hinder your enjoyment or appreciation of the present.

- You have more good times, and probably better ones, ahead. Learn to look back fondly without dwelling on what is over.

- Accept all of your past experiences as essential to making you who you are.

My good memories—vacations, the holidays—I have a lot of them. I remember a trip to Europe when my whole family went and we have pictures. . . . We went to Hawaii once. Those times you just remember fondly, you remember it as a time when we were together and we were happy with it. . . . And you don't really think about now. It's completely separate from it. You don't think, "Oh, why couldn't it still be," or, you know, none of that, just, "Yeah, that was a great time and I was really happy with it." Nothing is messed up, the memory is still there. It's still real, just like other things in the past that don't happen again. We can still enjoy it even though it's passing, as most things are.

MATT, Age 19

I didn't really miss that male figure, "Son, let's go play ball." I had that when I was younger. My dad and I used to go out in the yard. When I first had a big bike, my dad taught me how to ride it. I remember my dad pulling the sled up the hill. All my friends loved my dad. He was like one of the guys. That's cool sometimes, but other times, you don't know my dad. He's funny and he likes to tell jokes and stuff. So I remember a lot of good times even though he's kind of mad and bitter now.

JEFF, Age 19

I was pretty young. I don't remember much of the actual divorce. I do remember periods of time when we were together. My dad was in the Air Force and we went from place to place. We were in Panama for a while and my mom was there with us. I don't have very many images of the actual breakup. . . . I don't have too many memories of them breaking up. I have memories of them being together, not being together, being very separate, like when my dad finally got stationed in northern California. . . . My dad had visitation rights a weekend every month and two weeks or a month during the summer. When he was in other countries, like he was in the Philippines for a year, we didn't get to see him but once every six months. But when he lived in northern California, my dad actually drove down from northern California every time that it was his weekend. Six hours' drive I think it was. He'd spend the weekend with us and stay in a motel and drive back. During the summers he drove down to pick us up and take us back up there. He was very consistent about it. If it was his time, we were with him. He always wanted to be with us. I felt very good about that. I feel very good about my dad. And it's not like my mom was, "No, you can't pick them up," or anything like that. It was always like, "Okay, it's your turn." I felt pretty good about the time I got to spend with my dad. . . . I've only got a certain amount of time to do things in my life and I refuse to worry about things that are over.

STEVE, Age 25

47

Don't Report on One Parent to the Other— with Some Exceptions

The one thing that doesn't abide by majority rule is a person's conscience.

—HARPER LEE

We have already been over how you should not run messages between your parents. This is kind of the same idea. You should not be the person keeping tabs on your father for your mother or vice versa. Yeah, there are going to be times, pretty frequently, when you mention things that are going on with one parent to the other one. When you are trying to make arrangements for yourself that involve both of your parents, yeah, you are going to have to run between them a bit, unless they communicate especially well. They both have their own lives now, but they're still adults—if they need to know about what is going on with the other one they should be able to

214

just ask without having you be their eyes. Some things just aren't the business of a divorced parent.

On the other side of the same coin, if there are really bad things going down with one parent and it is affecting you, you need to tell your other parent. You know what this means. If you find yourself in situations that make you really uncomfortable, if you are being endangered in any way, if you are being harmed, you need to do some talking to someone in order to make it stop. Never keep any kind of abuse a secret. Even if you are really just confused about things that happen, things that they say or do, it would be better to get an explanation rather than to just suffer quietly, right?

Your parents have, in most circumstances, known each other better and longer than you have known them. You should be able to go to one to get advice on how to deal with the other, how to interpret things they say or do, and how to get help if it is needed. Your instincts will tell you when you are in a bad situation. You are the one who must, with help if need be, get yourself out of it. It is exactly this simple. There are no excuses for letting things that are bad for you continue. You won't be protecting anyone. You won't be saving anything. You may be losing a lot—even more than you realize.

Speak up. No one can help you if they don't know. If you can't go to your other parent about what's going on, find another responsible adult you can trust.

- Your parents have their own separate lives now. You should not tattle or keep tabs.

- There is a difference between tattling and seeking help in a serious situation. A *big* difference.

- Rule number one: Take care of you. Don't get caught or

stuck in situations that are bad for you. You can—you must—help yourself.

My mother, my brother, and I moved into an apartment. She went to work and then she went drinking and he and I were there alone. . . . She was also doing lots of drugs during that time, that was really bad, too, and bringing home lots of young guys. . . . I mean, it got much worse when my brother died. . . . We didn't tell Dad, "you know, Mom's not home ever." I mean, we could get money and my brother was almost 18, so he thought it was okay. It was just a big party for him. After my brother died it got really bad. She would be gone for like three weeks at a time and there was a woman who lived in the room that my brother used to live in, she was sort of there and sort of not; I was seeing a psychiatrist for my brother's death and I happened to mention that Mom doesn't hang around much. He said that was illegal and I couldn't live there anymore.

MELANIE, Age 20

My senior year of high school I had two jobs, and two jobs in the summer, and I took out student loans. My parents paid for nothing, so I had to take out loans. And I didn't know anything about it. So I filled out all these papers and I didn't understand it and I ended up paying really high interest. No one had really gone to school before me, so there was no one to help figure it out. My second year, the school told me I couldn't continue unless I came up with $4,000. So somehow I got my dad to take out a loan for me because I couldn't take out any more. And somehow he got the money. That was in September, and when I came home for Christmas, I found out that he'd gotten the money in October and he'd spent it. I went home and was yelling and screaming and he just sat there crying. Mom was *crying, I was crying. He just said how he was a bad person and he was so sorry. Now it's like it never happened. So I told my grandmother and she helped me a lot. I pushed myself through school. It may not be what they wanted me to do. But I found out what I wanted to do and I got myself through it.*

MARIANNE, Age 25

"It was when I was eleven about to turn twelve when they got separated. I think that they got divorced very soon after. I didn't even know when they got divorced. I wasn't paying attention really. There was too much else going on," says Melanie, 20. "Since I was like seven, I knew that my parents didn't love each other. My mother used to tell me all the time that she didn't love my father. It was obvious; they would fight a lot, they were always fighting. Looking back, she was always attacking him, but I always thought that Dad was being like a bad man, mean to Mom. She's an alcoholic and she would get drunk and they would fight about that.

"One night I was sitting in my room and their bedroom was right next to mine, and they were having this horrible fight, and my brother, who was six years older than me, he knew what was going on and he came in and was like, 'You know, I'll always take care of you, and I love you,' which was completely different. He was never like that. He was never demonstrative at all, so I knew that something was wrong. All of a sudden it got very quiet and then my mother came in and said, 'We're moving out.' So she went out and the next day got an apartment and we moved out that night.

"I really worshiped my mother a lot. I thought that she was just perfect. I remember her drinking a lot, but I don't remember being bothered by it except for two or three times when I just got really angry. Most of the time I was just really mean to my father. They would fight and I would just stand behind my mother with my hands on her shoulders and be like, 'Why are you picking on Mom, Dad?' So looking back it was really hellish, but when I was in it I didn't think that it was that bad. I was just so used to them fighting all the time that I thought that's just what parents did.

"We moved out on Halloween. Halloween until February twenty-seventh, which is the day my brother died, was just crazy. The day my mother, my brother, and I moved, that night my mother went out drinking and left us alone in the new apartment. That was pretty much the way it was, that pretty much set the tone. I think my dad found out after my brother died when it got really bad. I was seeing a psychiatrist for my brother's death and I happened to mention that Mom doesn't hang around much. He said that was illegal and I couldn't live there anymore. My father lived in another state and I couldn't go to school and live with him, so I had to find a place to live. So I went and I lived with my best friend for like two months. I lived in her house with her family.

"I lived with my dad and his girlfriend for, I guess, two years, maybe more. Then I went to boarding school. His girl-friend was already living there when I moved in. I had no idea that she even existed. I moved in and he was like, 'This is Susan, we're living together.' So we didn't get along for a really long time, which is why I went to boarding school, so I wouldn't have to be around them. Now I get along with them both, my father and his girlfriend, really well. Then, I was just like, 'Get out of my house.' My dad's girlfriend, her parents divorced when she was like twelve and she had to take total care of her mother. She said to me, 'There are going to be times when you really hate me and there are going to be times when I really hate you. Let's get over them, okay? Because I really love your dad.' It was true. Now I have a lot more sympathy for my father and what he was going through. I really hated him then and I was forced to live with him.

"Right after I moved out, my mom just took off and was in Alaska for a while and then she was in California and North Carolina. I had had to move out because she wasn't there. Basically my father and the psychiatrist made me move out. I don't think I would have done it on my own, I think I would have just stayed there. I wasn't really happy with my mother at that point, but I didn't want to hurt her. I knew it would be really devastating if I moved out.

"Now she lives in Maryland and she's finally sober. In the past five years she's gone through this cycle of deciding to stop drinking and going through programs and then starting to drink again. For like three years I didn't even speak to her. I wouldn't read her letters and I didn't speak to her, and then my father made me see her. They still talk, they get along really well. She has a job now. She's probably going to move south.

"Right before I came to college I went and I visited her in her apartment, which is like the most time I have spent with her since I moved out. It was really good but it was really painful. She showed me these poems that I wrote right after the divorce that were so intense and painful. It was so obvious to me that I was so confused and totally didn't know what to do, but I didn't feel like that then. I didn't think that I did, but looking back I was like, 'God, poor kid!' But now I think that she's finally okay, that she's finally straight. I think that she blames herself for my brother's death. Because he was in the process of moving out when he got in a car accident. He was in the hospital for like a week and he died there. But I think that she feels like she was forcing him to move out. And that's why he died. I didn't even know that apparently one of the reasons she was making him move out is that she woke up one night and he was holding a knife to her throat and was like, 'You f---ing bitch, I'm going to kill you,' so I don't know how she could blame herself, but I think she really does.

"I don't think my brother was ever fully together. I think that he really took the brunt of my parents' relationship, because he was old enough to really understand what was going on. I think that my mother put a lot of pressure on him without meaning to, to be good so that they could get divorced. I guess that right after they got divorced he started to get much worse and he started just stealing a lot, getting arrested a lot, and like drinking a lot. But I don't know if it was just a reaction to the divorce or just getting out of the house and being able to do these things which he was doing anyway, but we just didn't really know about. He was not ever stable, ever. It's like a soap opera. It's so weird that this could have all happened to me.

"It's been a long haul. I mean, I thought that I would get to a point where I would think that I was all better and then just be expressing how I felt in like different ways and like, I guess by sophomore year of high school I liked my parents, I didn't like my mother, but I liked my dad and his girlfriend. And I felt okay about things and I wasn't in so much pain about my brother's death. And then I got involved with this extremely abusive person. I think that coming out of that divorce I really felt that I wasn't good enough for anyone, and he'd do these things to me and I'd just take it. I'd think that I must deserve this, because people treat me badly, you know, my mother treated me badly. And so in the middle of that relationship I started going to therapy again and my counselor started going really far back and she said that she thought it all stemmed from my brother's death, my parent's divorcing, and my mother leaving. She put me on Prozac, which I think is really what helped the most, because now I can think about it and be sad about it and it's okay to be sad about it and not be like, 'Oh, I'm over that and I don't have to think about it now,' which is how I was for a long time and which I think is just unhealthy, you know.

"I think that it's so hard not to blame yourself in that situation. The main thing is just to find friends. Those who really care about you. Just surround yourself with people who really care about you and who will always be there to listen. Because the hardest part for me was that for the longest time I didn't have anyone that I could talk to about it. And there was just this shrink who I hated and who was really condescending, but I didn't have any friends. So I think that I would just say that it's okay to be upset, but you shouldn't run yourself into the ground just hating yourself for what's happened.

"It's really hard to find someone to talk to. For me, I wouldn't talk to someone that I didn't really like right away. I'd be really bratty to them. I finally found a therapist that I really trusted and I saw her for a year, and then I didn't go to her for about two years and then I called her up one really bad night and was like, 'Can I start seeing you again?' She was like very loving and not distant. She wouldn't hide her

personal life from me. She would tell me about the relationships between her husband and her children. I think that helped
a lot.

"My father has always talked very well of my mother. He's
never said anything bad about her except for stuff that I agree
with—like not bad stuff, just that she's a little spacey and
doesn't have her feet on the ground. When she was drunk she
would say really mean things about him, before and after she
moved out. She would accuse him of things that she was doing.
Like, she would say, 'You're having an affair,' when we all knew
that she was, or, 'You treat the children so badly,' when it was
really what she was doing. But now they both talk about each
other like they're really good people. I think that makes it a
lot easier. If they hated each other I wouldn't know what to
do. It's weird that they don't hate each other. I guess my
brother's death drew them together somehow. The divorce
probably wouldn't have been such a big deal if there hadn't
been all of this other stuff going on at the same time.

"The biggest thing that I learned from their divorce is that
my parents are real people. Real people make all kinds of
mistakes, and real people get hurt by things. I think that I had
to find it out much faster than most kids do. Everything they
do isn't thought out and planned. In retrospect my family just
became people all of a sudden. I didn't know that when I
was little."

48

Do Your Part to Keep Up a Good Relationship with Your Nonresident Parent

Effort is only effort when it begins to hurt.

—José Ortega y Gasset

If you have read this far, I hope one point is clear: Your parents are both still your parents. Neither you nor they can do anything about this. It's a fact of biology and sociology and probably a few other ologies.

Even if you don't especially like or get along with the parent you are not living with, he or she is just as much a part of you and who you are as your resident parent. For the most part, people are better off when they keep in touch with the people they are related to and who had something to do with their being born in the first place. Sure, there are times and situations in which everyone is better off, especially the kids, not seeing much of a close relative who only makes trouble. In general, however, it is a good idea not to cut those ties.

The worst thing that you can do to yourself is to act rashly and end up regretting what you have done. Even if your parent is not doing his or her part, you need to give that parent the benefit of the doubt for as long as you reasonably can. If they aren't trying to keep in touch with you, and you would like to keep up a good relationship with them, go ahead. Call or write and tell them you want to see them. Let them know they matter to you until they come around and start doing their part right. Maybe they are just feeling a little worthless these days, given what they are going through or have been through. They can't be in control of everything, and they might not know that you really want to keep in touch. Maybe they don't know what they're doing (does *anybody* really know what they are doing?). Fact of life: They're playing it by ear, just like we all are. You are extremely lucky if you don't have trouble traversing the distance between you and your nonresident parent.

The thing that you should most try to avoid in this kind of a situation is being the bad guy. Make sure, above all else, that you are not the one to make things strange. Yeah, they're supposed to be the adults. It is kind of their responsibility to make sure that things are going well, that they are keeping on top of things, maintaining a healthy relationship with their children, but if it's clear that they are just not getting the job done, don't make it worse by acting out all your nastiest feelings. Also, you *do* have responsibilities to your folks, because you are their offspring. They can't keep on top of things if you aren't doing your part.

Doing your part does not mean that you have to do it all, just that you shouldn't make things more difficult than they already are. If your parent tells you to come over whenever you feel like it, don't wait for a formal invitation. Go over occasionally, even if it's just for a few minutes, even when you're thinking you might as well just go home. If they have arranged to call you at a certain time, be there. Make nice, ask them how they're doing, be interested, treat them like your parents and not some infernal obligation. Invite them to your school events or whatever. You can make it easier to be on good terms if you are a bit flexible and if you are really willing to help make it work. As long as you can see that they are trying at all, your efforts will be worthwhile.

- Don't snub your nonresident parent because he or she has disappointed you. This is a relationship you can't blow off easily.

- No matter who you live with, you still have two parents. Maybe one of them needs to be reminded of this.

- They might think you don't even want to relate to them. Don't let them think that if it isn't true.

My father is the one who really takes care of it. If I call my mother up and tell her I need something she'll say, "I'm sorry, I just got back from Jamaica." And I'll have to call my father about it. She's just kind of living it up. It wasn't that way when they were together, but she wasn't real involved. She always had her attention on other things. It just seems really random when it suddenly occurs to her that she should say something motherly. I used to not like to be around my father very much. He's very eccentric. He always said that he wished we had been closer, but I think that was mostly my doing. So divorce has changed my relationship with both of them. My mother was never the big nurturing mother. I was left alone a lot as far as that goes, but at least we've gotten a friendship between us.

KIMBERLY, Age 21

I think it also helped that when I was in high school my dad was out of the Air Force and he tried to be as close with us as possible. He lived in the same city we lived in with my mom by then, and we'd go and visit him all the time, any time we wanted to. Even when I was in the Navy and I went home to visit my friends and parents in California, I could go from one house to the other, stay at my dad's for a few days, and still see my friends because they lived so close together. Luckily, my parents have good communication.

STEVE, Age 25

49

Make the Effort to Stay in Touch with the Relatives You Like

In a full heart there is room for everything, and in an empty heart there is room for nothing.

—ANTONIO PORCHIA

Most people don't get to pick and choose what parts of their families they are going to keep around. When families stay together, it is harder to escape them. Don't take this lightly. No matter how much most of us would love to just walk away from some of the more embarrassing branches of our family trees, it's a good thing that it isn't easy.

Family is a great thing when you think about it. It is an unconditional tie to some interesting people. Why blow them off when that can easily be avoided with a couple of well-timed phone calls? Just like with your parents, you are related to all of these folks for your whole life. They are just as related to you even if you don't see them very often, even if you weren't in touch frequently before all of the strange custody and division of holiday time went on.

Family can be a fickle thing. Sometimes people figure that if your parents aren't related to each other anymore, you are not related anymore either. Kids can get lumped in with the ex-spouse, even though this is a stupid division. Legally and biologically you are just as related to them as before; sometimes they don't understand that, no matter how simple it seems to you.

It also sometimes happens that they are so angry about all of the stuff that went on in an ugly divorce that they don't want to have anything to do with the other side of the family, you included. This is equally stupid and a bit more hurtful. Just make sure that you are not the one blocking relations unless you know that's how you want it to be.

Bad reasons for excluding relatives include, but are not limited to: They are cheap, they smell, they cook strange food, their kids are obnoxious, they live far away, and it's their job to keep in touch with me. The price of a stamp is negligible and you can probably get at least one of your parents to spring for the price of a phone call once in a while.

Families are cool. You've got two separate ones now, divided along some pretty clear and distinct lines, and if your parents have remarried, you may have some auxiliary family, too. If your relatives don't know what to do about these lines, if they don't know how to handle things, tell them. If you've noticed that your mother's parents don't call you at your father's house and you'd like them to, tell them that it's okay to call you there. You can be subtle if you want: "I'll be at my dad's this weekend, you can call me there anytime before eleven o'clock. I should be home all night." You get the gist. Not subtle, but still within the bounds of courtesy and kindness: "I've noticed that you don't call us at Mom's house since the divorce. I'd really like it if you did. She won't be rude, I promise." They should be able to handle a ten-second conversation with their ex-in-law on the way to talking to you.

If your relatives don't hassle you and feel totally comfortable dealing with your parents, that's wonderful. You're very lucky. And if like many people you've suddenly come into a whole new family of stepgrandparents, stepaunts, and stepuncles who are thrilled to know you, all the better. The more the merrier and all that. The world is full of interesting people. It's fun to be related to some of them. There's no such thing as too much love.

- Don't let your family ties go too easily. Make at least some effort to keep up with people you care about, even if they are not immediately making the effort to keep up with you.

- You are still related to everyone that you were ever related to, and maybe now you're related to some other cool people. It is usually valuable for you to keep up with them.

- You don't have to follow them around or anything, just don't be the one who cuts off contact unless you are sure that you want it to be that way.

For a while, because my uncles and my grandfather disowned us (and I was very close to my grandfather), I remember thinking one time that I don't trust men, because of my father, my uncles, my grandfather. But then I thought, I'm denying myself a happiness I could have. So I'm growing up now. Sometimes I didn't know if I'd take those relatives who disowned us back. I'd try to forgive, but then I felt like, Okay, I forgive you, but stay away from me. I don't want to be hurt again. The funny thing is, when they finally did get in touch with us again, I was incredibly happy. I love them.

LISA, Age 19

My father's side of the family doesn't really talk to us anymore. They seem to have decided that my brothers and I are related to my mother and not to them. They're wrong, but I can't explain that to them. I write to them sometimes; it's easier now that I'm away at school, but I don't really know them anymore. I'm still related to my dad, so I am still related to them, but it doesn't seem like they see it that way. It's kind of sad that they don't know who I am anymore. A lot of things have gone on and I've changed a lot since my parents split up. I'm sorry that they don't seem to want to be any part of it. I just don't want it to be my fault that we don't know each other.

Nora, Age 20

My mother's parents still like my dad. They still give him Christmas presents. His parents, well, like this summer my mom, my brother, and I went over there for dinner, without my dad. They're still friendly and civil and very nice. And my grandparents, both sets, are friends with each other still; they do everything together. They've always run in the same social circle. But my dad did remarry and that's kind of weird. My mom's parents pretty much just choose to ignore Dad's new wife, you know, as if she doesn't exist. . . . My dad's aunt, my grandfather's older sister, I love her to death, she's wonderful, but she has taken to my dad's new wife and has decided to completely ignore my mother—which is really hard because my mom and her were always very close—and I really respect her and love her and it hurts me that she won't acknowledge the fact that my mother is still alive. It's a sore spot with me.

Donna, Age 20

50

Divorce Isn't Hereditary

Every generation goes someplace bigger.

—Faith Sullivan

Most people who have been a part of a divorce can't help but wonder about the reliability, strength, and endurance of marriage. What makes it work or not work?

The kids of divorced couples usually have gotten a rare glimpse into divorce from both sides. The two parties in the dispute have a connection through this young person who is still dependent on them. Not a fun spot for the kid to occupy.

Naturally, it's a situation that tends to confuse, frustrate, and muddle the children of divorce. The bond between their parents, supposedly made for life, has been broken. The children feel left out, not a part of what's going on. There is nothing that they can do to affect the situation. They are helpless and don't understand how this came about or what's going to happen next, even though they are right at the center of it.

So why get married at all? Why make that kind of bond with someone if it only leads to all the trouble and pain of divorce further down the road? What is the redeeming feature of this plan?

These are the thoughts of the people we have talked to. Yet, eventually, most of them have decided that they do in fact plan on getting married and they all say that when it happens to them, it will be for real. It sounds kind of unrealistic. That the kids of the people who couldn't make it work are going to make it work may not sound like a good bet, especially with the divorce rate as high as it is.

But these kids have also seen what happens when people stop being able to communicate or when people are dishonest about their feelings. They know how much it hurts when a loving relationship turns sour. They don't want to set themselves up for that; they really believe that they can make marriage work when it is their turn. They're not planning a series of marriages. They just want to work on one and keep it working. Maybe their experience with divorce will give them some of the equipment they need to succeed.

- Your parents' mistakes are just that, your parents'. You are not destined to repeat them.

- You have been given a good opportunity to look at human relationships from an intimate standpoint. Pay attention. You can learn a lot.

- Since you know a lot about what can go wrong in a relationship, you also know more about what you need to make it work.

All in all my dad's a good person except that I don't want to be like him in the fact that he was married three times. Once I get married, that's it. When we say "till death do us part" that means her. I don't want to get out of it and neither does she. At first I was like, "Marriage, big deal, so what? You get divorced." Now, as I get older I see it as, when I select that woman that I'm going to marry, I mean she's going to mother my children. She's going to be very special, right? And once we get married, it's going to be forever. And I don't want to be like my dad with kids in one state and kids in another.

ROB, Age 20

Over the years I've realized in a lot of ways why their marriage didn't work. . . . The most important thing to me in my life is family and I'm never going to have a marriage that fails. I've learned so much from what my parents went through that I just don't see my marriage ever failing. . . . They got married right out of college and they were both pretty young, and I don't know how much time they really took to get to know each other. I don't know how much time they took to establish communication before they got married, and I think that probably had a lot to do with it. I've already been going out with my girlfriend longer than my parents knew each other when they got married. They met sophomore year of college and they got married right after college. And I've been going out with Amy for three years now. We're not even thinking about getting married until way after she graduates. That's going to be a long time and I think that's important.

NICK, Age 20

My parents are not me. If I were giving advice to someone whose parents are getting divorced I'd say not to worry about it. A lot of people go through it and you just have to realize that there's nothing you can do about it. There's nothing you can do to make the situation better. I mean, deal with it, but there's nothing you can do to stop it. Everything will be all right. It happens to plenty of people. You're going to get through it—you have to get through it. There's nothing else you can do.

DONNA, Age 20

If you would like to tell us your story or share a bit of advice, we would be glad to hear from you. Please write to us c/o Avon Books, 1350 Avenue of the Americas, New York, New York 10019.

BETH BARUCH JOSELOW, mother of Thea, Ethan, and Gabe, was divorced in 1991. She is a poet, playwright, and assistant professor of academic studies at The Corcoran School of Art in Washington, D.C., where she lives with her children and her husband, Tom Mandel. Her book, *Life Lessons: 50 Things I Learned from My Divorce,* was published by Avon Books in 1994. Her work also has been published in *Ladies' Home Journal, The Washington Post, Washington Review of the Arts,* and elsewhere.

THEA JOSELOW is in the class of 1996 at Oberlin College in Oberlin, Ohio. She has been a writer all her life and at times has found employment as a coffee shop worker, bookstore salesperson, camp counselor, and baby-sitter. She has two younger brothers and many friends.